HIGHWAY
AMERICA'S ENDLESS DREAM

PHOTOGRAPHS
JEFF BROUWS

TEXT
BERND POLSTER
PHIL PATTON

HIGHWAY

AMERICA'S ENDLESS DREAM

STEWART, TABORI & CHANG
NEW YORK

Parking Lot | **Vega, Texas** | 1991

CONTENTS

PHOTOGRAPHERS IN THE DRIVER'S SEAT

BY BERND POLSTER

Slowly we drove down the highway through a wide expanse. In the distance, the silhouette of a mountain chain appeared like a phantom, but so infinitely far away that my feeling for distance failed me. Although we were constantly driving toward them, the peaks on the horizon never seemed to come any closer. To this day you can still see that this lunar landscape was once the bed of a dried-up prehistoric ocean. And as the highway took us right into the heart of it, the big pale blue sky became even bigger. Against the light, the asphalt resembled a wide river, a shimmering metallic band on which we glided through the valley without a sound.

This almost unreal piece of earth we were crossing was the Mojave Desert, a landscape composed of dust and rock where the temperature doesn't even come close to bearable until night falls and the coyotes start to howl. It was this extreme landscape that formed a natural obstacle for America's pioneer highway, the famous Route 66, the first road to traverse the continent from east to west.

It wasn't until the beginning of the Thirties that the sandy field-paths that still fearfully clung to the old railroad tracks were turned into a passable gravel road. Even to the Oklahoma and Arkansas farmers who, during the depths of the Depression, were California-bound in search of work, the desert presented the last great barrier and the new road crossing it became the "highway to Heaven."

In the Fifties, it was considered chic to follow in the tracks of the poor Okies and Arkies. Weekend adventurers would drive out into the desert, hanging water bags from their bumpers and constantly checking to make sure that their gas tanks and radiators were filled to the brim. Motels opened in the small "food-n-gas" communities along the highway and had names like Golden West or Wigwam and featured monstrous neon signs easily spotted from miles away. "Roadside" came to mean pioneer spirit, mobility, and free enterprise.

AN AMERICAN DREAM SEEMED TO BECOME REALITY IN THE DUST OF THE ROAD.

While filming *Bagdad Cafe* in the mid-Eighties, the crew had scouted for a dreary motel rest-stop site and found it along a piece of Route 66 that passed through the Mojave Desert. Where once this road stretched gloriously, its lights were now long extinguished. And it is this melancholy mood of desolation that finds its way into the film.

This same mood is also imparted through the numerous images in this book taken by photographer Jeff Brouws, whose images are the result of his journey across hundreds of thousands of miles of American highway and whose themes cannot be found in any brochures. Well-known clichés of the "big-sky cowboy country" are rarely included, and when they are, they are intended to communicate an irony.

Many of the places that Brouws has photographed look like they won't be there tomorrow: the deserted cafe with the toppled barstools, the dried-up desert gas station, or the motel sign with its peeled paint. There is a patina of history so hyper-realistic that you feel as if you can almost scrape it off, and in many of his pictures time seems to have frozen.

WITH THEIR MAGICAL CONTRASTS OF LIGHT AND EXTREME PERSPECTIVES, BROUWS'S PHOTOGRAPHS OF CARS IN MOTION SEEM LIKE STILLS FROM A FILM CLIP, A YET-TO-BE-SEEN ROAD MOVIE.

Brouws's photographs were taken exclusively using a medium-format camera and are presented in three portfolios. They show long series of pictures that capture the atmosphere of highways found in all corners of the United States. There are also important thematic aspects portrayed in concentrated dossiers of text and image. Seven sequences of photos and commentary cover several topics: "Lanes," what America drives on; "Signs," the folk art that zooms past the eye; "Gas Stations" and "Drive-ins," the consumer spots for people and their vehicles; "Passers-by," the people who live and make their living off the highway; "Mainstreet," the heart of the country still beating in our memory; and finally, "Ruins," the relics of an era that is crumbling along the side of the highway.

The scenes depicted in Jeff Brouws's photographs are for the most part unpopulated and filled with melancholy. In their simple construction and quiet atmosphere, they are reminiscent of the world of painter Edward Hopper, who not only helped shape the view of the American roadside, but who also influenced contemporary film and photography.

During the Depression, the government's Farm Security Administration (FSA) authorized a project under whose auspices photographers spent years traveling the country with car and camera in order to document the plight of the people. Roy Stryker, the FSA project director, demanded an uncompromising documentary style. As a result, closeups of the nation's condition were made.

Many of the photographers who participated in this project from the outset, such as Dorothea Lange and Walker Evans, later became famous; Lange and Evans are today considered extremely important artists. Later, additional, as yet unknown, photographers joined the group. Among them were Jack Delano, Russell Lee, and Marion Post Wolcott. The roads they traveled provided the favored themes of these FSA photographers. During that same time, newly founded American magazines like *LIFE* and *Look* began featuring a breakthrough reporting style based on photography. It was through this medium, and the photographers who provided the gripping images, that road culture became absorbed into a collective visual memory and became a part of folklore; America's intimate relationship to its highways had found its aesthetic counterpart.

The American public, already geared to mobility, welcomed the quick medium of photography and the car became its natural resource. The photographer at the wheel is a typically American phenomenon. He is the protagonist who gathers his impressions while driving by. A selection of these historic black-and-white photographs, archived in Library of Congress, illustrate the book's two essays on highway history and form an important aspect of Brouws's work.

In the book's first essay, "The Road to Nowhere," famed highway chronicler Phil Patton traces the myth of the open road, while the second essay, "Movies Through the Windshield," follows the growth of American roadside culture and shows how eventually even Europeans caught on-the-road fever through films such as *Easy Rider; Paris, Texas;* and *Thelma and Louise.*

Highway 14 | **Sylmar, California** | 1996

The Golden West Motel l Reno, Nevada l 1996

Grain Elevator I **U.S. 66, Texas** I 1991

Skyline I **Cleveland, Ohio** I 1995

Parking Meter | Modesto, California | 1994

DON'T SPEAK WITH YOUR BANKING FRIENDS OR YOUR CHAMBER OF COMMERCE FRIENDS, BUT SPECIALIZE IN THE GASOLINE STATION MEN, THE SMALL RESTAURANT KEEPER, AND FARMERS YOU MEET BY THE WAYSIDE...

FRANKLIN D. ROOSEVELT

Gas Station Attendant I **South Dakota** I 1992

The Golden Motel | **Valmy, Nevada** | 1996

Abandoned Motel Room I **Shamrock, Texas** I 1993

Interstate 5 | **Castaic, California** | 1996

The Mint Bar | **Sheridan, Wyoming** | 1992

THE AVERAGE AMERICAN SPENDS A LOT OF HIS LEISURE TIME CRUISING THE HIGHWAY. THAT'S WHY THE GAS STATIONS, ROADS, MOTELS, AND REMOTE INNS ARE AMERICAN THROUGH AND THROUGH.

SIMONE DE BEAUVOIR

Abandoned Gas Station I **Delano, California** I 1989

Neon Sign I **U.S. 66, Oklahoma** I 1991

Gas Station Attendant | **Montana** | 1992

The Morris Hotel | Reno, Nevada | 1995

Motel Parking Lot I **Reno, Nevada** I 1995

YOU LOOK UP THE HIGHWAY AND IT IS STRAIGHT FOR MILES, COMING AT YOU, WITH THE BLACK LINE DOWN THE CENTER COMING AT YOU AND AT YOU, BLACK AND SLICK...

Robert Penn Warren

U.S. 99 I Bakersfield, California I 1996

Roadside Cafe I **Battle Mountain, Nevada** I 1996

Car Fire | **Interstate 40, California** | 1995

The El Morocco Motel I **Bakersfield, California** I 1994

Gas Station I **Inyokern, California** I 1990

ROAD TO NOWHERE

BY PHIL PATTON

Interstates/inner states: It's the right pun. The name of America's superhighway system suggests connections, but the effect of the system is to foster and convey all sorts of individual and collective emotions. It is the nervous system of the body politic, the body economic, the body cultural. "Oh Public Road," Whitman intoned long before the first cloverleaf sprouted among the leaves of grass, "you express me better than I can express myself!"

In America, the driver between political states is also the driver between states of mind. Those who drive are often alone, often between, lives. They are abandoning old identities and looking for new ones, but are most themselves in the interval. Some drive to remember, others to forget.

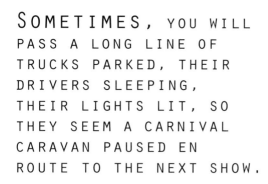

We speak of the American "way" of life, not the American "form" of life. As John Steinbeck wrote of the Okies: "The highway was their home, and movement their means of expression."

We speak of "voting with your feet"—moving to a state or city you liked better—but could add, "voting with your wheels." Now America has a new motor voter law that ties voter registration to the production of driver's licenses—that common requirement for credit as well. The driver's license is a virtual document of American citizenship, the ticket to ride the highway.

According to American music, constant travel and living on the road can also become an intoxication, an addiction heard in Merle Haggard's *White Line Fever,* in which he sings "the years keep flying by like high line poles."

Fever or calm—both live on the American highway. There's a peace on the road, a sense of self containment in one's cockpit that the hours of driving bring on. The truckers become your friends, and as dusk settles and their long metal trailers begin to go soft in the headlights that ignite their quilted and damascened skins, the big rectangles seem light and airy as foil. The red lights along their length become festive and happy.

SOMETIMES, YOU WILL PASS A LONG LINE OF TRUCKS PARKED, THEIR DRIVERS SLEEPING, THEIR LIGHTS LIT, SO THEY SEEM A CARNIVAL CARAVAN PAUSED EN ROUTE TO THE NEXT SHOW.

The most celebrated road in America, the one closest to the American heart, is Woody Guthrie and John Steinbeck's Route 66, but the closest to the American soul is Robert Johnson and Elmore James's Highway 61, the road of escape, the road from agriculture to industry, from the South to the North, the primitive to the civilized.

Highway 61 runs from Jackson Square in New Orleans (once site of a slave market) north through Vicksburg, Memphis, St. Louis and on to Canada. Sixty-one is a road of opportunity too, but a different one: it represents a road of escape for African Americans from the Mississippi Delta and sharecropping to factory work in the North, in Chicago and Detroit. Highway 61 crosses

Highway 49 in Clarksdale, Mississippi—the center of blues culture—to form the most famous crossroads in the area. It also bears the heavy freight of the meaning of the blues, derived from hoodoo and African legend. The blues is obsessed with the highway—from *Big Road Blues* to *Down the Dirt Road Blues* to *Key to the Highway* (the joke here is that even a poor sharecropper needs no key to the highway, for this is not the king's but the people's highway, requiring not even the car key but simply a bus ticket or just a hitchhiker's thumb to ride.)

The song touches on the democratic, open nature of the American road, right up to the superhighways. In Europe, the fast and slow lanes represent a virtual first and second class system of automobiles, echoing that of the railroad. Slower, cheaper cars give way to faster ones. But just as America abandoned rail classes, it also left any driver to choose any lane—an often maddening experience for the driver stuck behind the dawdling economy car in the passing lane.

Highway 61 carried Elvis and Ike Turner to Memphis, it took Muddy Waters and Elmore James north to Chicago, where they learned to plug their guitars in to electricity—and their music into the main cultural power grid of America. And 61 is the highway of the bluesman who deals with the devil and flees "the hellhound on his trail."

The blues highway ends in *Crossroads Blues,* and in Robert Johnson's sung request to be buried by the side of the highway, so his old evil spirit can "take a Greyhound bus and ride." As the destination for his imaginary rides, Johnson combines "sweet home Chicago" with the magic land of California toward which 66 runs. (The geography is strictly symbolic in his lyrics.) What made Highway 61 different is that it ran in both directions spiritually as well; north toward freedom, and south toward discovery, to inspire

people like Bob Dylan—who grew up as Robert Zimmerman a few miles from 61 in Minnesota—to write *Highway 61 Revisited.* Highway 61 is a darker vision of America, the cultural cross roads (wholly theoretical, since their pavements never actually merge) where 61 meets 66.

Or does the blues highway end in Aretha Franklin's *Freeway of Love,* on the way to San Jose in a pink Cadillac, an image of mainstream opportunity. Along the way, one can see the evolution of blues toward rock-and-roll in the succession of songs from Robert Johnson's *Terraplane Blues* to *Rocket 88,* an homage to an Oldsmobile often considered the first true rock-and-roll song, and thence to Chuck Berry's *Maybelline* and Prince's *Little Red Corvette.* And in early country and western music the road figures as a Bunyan-like course to sin or redemption: *Lost Highway* is the most significant title here.

Until the telegraph, roads were a means of communication as well as transportation. They brought news from the far reaches of the empire, and delivered the message of military power and control. There were differences in speed, more marked as time went on. The Pony Express could move much faster but the means of delivery was the same.

In this country, the first "improved" roads were dedicated to the post. But by the mid-twentieth century they had places to BE. Real estate men began to speak of highways that had become "saturated," their sides and interchanges "built to capacity." Roads were no longer even primarily means of transportation, they were patterns for location.

Above all, American roads are public spaces. "Public Road," Whitman's inelegant, bureaucratic term, was current from the 1880s to the 1960s. Before this century, public roads were mostly inferior substitutes for private ones. The most sophisticated roads of the nineteenth century were private turnpikes, and the railroads were owned by giant corporations. Only the automobile made all roads public. Like television, American highways are a national network, a mass medium. Driving, in fact, has been studied by psychologists as a process not unlike watching television.

AS WE BEMOAN THE EFFECTS OF TELEVISION, WE ALSO LAMENT THE EFFECTS OF MODERN HIGHWAYS WITH ALMOST THE SAME INTENSITY WITH WHICH WE DEVOTE OURSELVES TO THEM.

They have had monstrous side effects. They have often rolled, like some gigantic version of the machines that built them, through cities, splitting communities off into ghettos, displacing people, and crushing the intimacies of old cities with a scale taken from dreams of the wide-open spaces. They have become a symbol of the American distrust and dislike for the city.

And yet American roads are a reservation of individuality and privacy. Americans have gone on the road to find America and find themselves, following in the naïve Whitmanesque mode. The song of the open road is also the song of the self, a song of elusive identity, of blue skies, blue roads, and the blues.

While promising to bring us closer, highways in fact cater to our sense of separateness. The quintessential American who takes the lost highway—like the basic country singer who is constantly singing about moving on down the road—is a connoisseur of a special loneliness. The man out to see the U.S.A. in his Chevrolet, with or without family, cultivates a sense of alienation. His vacations are a continual reenactment of discovery and exploration, and for discovery, we

PACKAGE DELIVERY SERVICE. COMBINATION POST OFFICE AND GAS STATION IN PIE TOWN, NEW MEXICO.

DREARY OMEN. SANDSTORM BLOWING
ACROSS THE FLAT LAND. PANHANDLE,
TEXAS.

CIGARETTES, FOOD AND AMMUNITION.
GENERAL STORE ON HIGHWAY 60. DATIL
MOUNTAINS, NEW MEXICO.

must refresh our sense of being aliens, nurture our otherness.

Ultimately, any set of roads embodies a philosophy, a "way." How many American dreamers, in search of the national spirit and ultimately themselves, have taken to the road with the same bluster as Whitman, to find Truth and the Way and Ourselves and Themselves? Writers and tourists both have taken to the road, dedicated to the proposition that on the road the traveler must inevitably, eventually, meet himself. "To know the universe itself as road" Whitman writes—a tall order, a romantic ambition, an American dream.

The road's cult of the individual approaches the pathological. American society has found the death by accident of some fifty thousand people a year on the road an acceptable price to pay for preserving the individuality of the driver on the common ground of the highway. (The cumulative accident total long ago passed the common comparison of "more than in all wars the United States has fought.") And we struggle along blindly in the face of immutable but incomprehensible laws by which each new highway seems to fill to capacity as soon as we can complete it. And yet we continue to dream of new highways, safe and free flowing open roads. For in America, highways are much more than a means of transportation. They come as close as anything we have to a central national space. They are a national promenade, "America's Main Street," and a medium in which grows the carnival of individual life and enterprise.

The American obsession with transportation comes naturally to a country so vast. But in the U.S. the transportation has come before the things to transport; the cities were located on the transportation system rather than the transportation among the cities. Each new system of transportation shaped the economic and social landscape more than it was shaped by it.

Rivers may have sited cities in Europe, but here the railroads sited them—Chicago and Atlanta, among others. More recently, superhighways have escaped old city sites to replace them with ring developments. The "edge cities" Joel Garreau wrote about in a book of the same name are suburbs that have supplanted cities.

American roads were built to escape cities—Jefferson's fear of them is well known and as president he personally directed the forging of the Natchez Trace into the new Louisiana Purchase. More importantly, he laid out the great grid of land organization that directed the settlement of the West and the admission of new states. Roads were part of the effort.

The establishment of the grid had other, more subtle but persistent consequences. Beginning in 1916 with the first federal highway aid, the topic of a national network of highways arose; and it was the grid—however reshaped by the competing topologies of politics, economics, and geography—that served as a basis for all the versions of such networks, down to the final Interstate map.

Well before the land ordinances, American city planning, beginning with William Penn's Philadelphia, adopted the grid, mostly with the aim of retaining green, open land in the city, in contrast to dank, dark London. The most striking image of the gridded city is the famous engraving made of Savannah, Georgia, as laid out by James Oglethorpe. Like planting beds in a classical garden, the blocks of Savannah, some reserved for parks, seem to have been stamped out by some giant press among the tall pines that rise with the same linear geometry as the streets. Grid in the city, grid over the country: these patterns dictated a necessary connection between urban street and rural highway. The grid, as the organizing principle for most cities, also tied them directly to the national highway grid.

Jean-Paul Sartre once observed that while European streets typically end in some enclosed space, the straight

ONE-HORSE-POWER CARRIAGE IN FRONT OF A NEW ENGLAND GENERAL STORE. GRAYSVILLE, VERMONT.

streets of the American city seem to run on forever, opening the very heart of the city up to the horizon and denying it the separation and special status of a Paris, Rome, or London. In those centers the roads of the country converge, but in America the urban grid disperses the city into the country.

AMERICAN STREETS, SARTRE ARGUED, "ARE NOT SOBER LITTLE WALKS CLOSED IN BETWEEN HOUSES, BUT NATIONAL HIGHWAYS. THE MOMENT YOU SET FOOT ON ONE OF THEM, YOU UNDERSTAND THAT IT HAS TO GO ON TO BOSTON OR CHICAGO."

In 1948 Robert Frank photographed a major Manhattan cross street, probably 42nd Street. In the center of the picture is a white line down the middle of the road, disappearing into the distance in a virtuoso demonstration of perspective. Almost all of the picture is filled with pavement; only at the top edges, in perhaps a tenth of its surface, does the sidewalk and its pedestrian life, shops, and signs appear, the bustle reduced as if to a distant noise. The photograph is an urban parody of the famous shots by Dorothea Lange and Frank himself of straight, receding highways disappearing across the western plains, but one that establishes something in common between the two kinds of road. It suggests the identity of American urban geometry with rural geometry, the connections of all the grids.

No wonder that the superhighway builders would venture into the city as if the roads they built across Kansas farmland or New Mexico desert could simply be transplanted to the city, perhaps raised on piles if necessary, to allow their builders to ignore the local landscape

UNDER THE ASPHALT LIES THE BEACH. HIGHWAY 98 ALONG THE GULF OF MEXICO. PENSACOLA, FLORIDA.

the same way they could ignore the landscape of the wide open spaces. Both landscapes were organized on grids, but they were different grids, and the result was a debilitating conflict of scales.

Even in Los Angeles, the first city of freeways, the superhighways were organized into a loose grid. But it was a grid compatible with the street grid. The classic view of Los Angeles at night confirms the fact: seen from the hills around it, the city spreads out in a great flat reticule of lights. By contrast with eastern cities in which freeways were imposed over the grid as spokes and rims, the L.A. freeways themselves form a grid integrated into the small-scale grid of the blocks.

BUT SOME OF THE BEST VIEWS OF THE AMERICAN ROAD COME FROM FOREIGN VISITORS, TO WHOM IT ALL SEEMS BRIGHT AND STRANGE.

In Vladimir Nabokov's novel *Lolita,* road culture becomes self-conscious, ironic. The book presents a view of the road and of the whole vast country. The roads unfold as a realm for individual projection, for solipsistic recreation, with their random elements organized by the tortured mind of the narrator and hero. The whole landscape becomes a mock romantic register for Humbert's individual emotions.

"How many small dead-of-night towns I have seen. Neon lights flickered twice slower than my heart." His fear takes the form of a huge tractor-trailer, and elsewhere that of a mysterious Aztec-red sedan. *Lolita* also provides one of the best documents we have of the American road before the advent of the superhighways. It is filled with a series of mock-epic catalogs, a takeoff of the AAA Guides Humbert uses to plot the trip: "...all those Sunset Motels, U-Beams, Hillcrest Courts, Pine View

THE LIGHTS OF a small town. Gas stations and bar along the highway. Childersburg, Alabama.

Courts, Mountain View Courts, Skyline Courts, Park Plaza Courts, Green Acres, Mac's Courts."

In what can be read as a broad and perverse parody of the devices millions of parents have used to keep their kids quiet in the backseat, Humbert uses roadside attractions to help keep Lolita in his thrall, setting up each of them, with the aid of roadside signs indicating their distance, as one more putative goal of the endless journey.

"Every morning during our yearlong travels I had to devise some expectation, some special point in space and time for her to look forward to...a lighthouse in Virginia, a natural cave in Arkansas converted to a cafe, a collection of guns and violins somewhere in Oklahoma, a replica of the Grotto of Lourdes in Louisiana, shabby photographs of the bonanza mining period in the local museum of a Rocky Mountain resort, anything whatsoever—but it had to be there, in front of us, like a fixed star, although as likely as Lo would feign gagging as soon as we got to it."

Nabokov notes the cute toilet signs "Guys-Gals, John-Jane, Jack-Jill, and even Bucks-Does." The observation, for all the madness of the narrator, is Nabokov's observation: detailed and almost scientific, as befits a professional lepidopterist who recorded most of it during thousands of miles of summer travel during the late Forties and early Fifties, in pursuit of butterflies.

But Nabokov himself never learned to drive. His wife was at the wheel. What the driver and the passenger see are phenomenologically different. Nabokov's was the view from the passenger seat.

And so *Lolita* is made up of a catalog of observations. It is not concerned with the flow of the road, the dynamic of movement that is Jack Kerouac's concern. *On the Road,* by contrast, is a continuum of discoveries and departures. Kerouac writes with his head turned toward the land-scape disappearing behind him. His book is an essay on the phenomenology of pure driving, of encounter and

FUEL FOR THE "MOTOR MARATHON."
SERVICE STATION ON MAIN STREET,
CADDO, OKLAHOMA.

WAVY LINES. HIGHWAY 97 RUNS
ACROSS THE COLUMBIA RIVER GORGE.
KLICKETAT COUNTY, WASHINGTON.

abandonment. In *Lolita,* Humbert is a cool and distant, if cynical and desperate, observer who uses precision and irony to keep his emotions at bay. But in *On the Road* the emotion overflows in a stream of present participles.

In Kerouac the pretense of a goal is dropped almost completely. His heroes are driving nowhere in particular—just "to the Coast" or back, which is the same as somewhere in general. They are existential drivers seeking inner states before the Interstates. The driver without a destination is kin to the rebel without a cause.

"What is that feeling when you're driving away from people and they recede on the plain until you see their specks dispersing? It's the too-huge world vaulting us, and it's good-bye. But we lean forward to the next crazy venture beneath the skies," he wrote.

Kerouac's heroes always drive well, but too fast, taking some imagined existential risk for discovery. Speed and danger are part of the thrill of Kerouac's road, the heat and pressure in which the driver can forget himself and concentrate only on the beat of the wheels.

The superhighways gradually domesticated the wilderness of the old roads, settling and closing the highway frontier, eliminating the possibilities for escape. But the creation of the superhighway also strengthened the American fascination with the roadside, adding to its exclamatory, cataloging, wondering tone an elegiac haze.

The road figured in American politics and culture as an alternative to the railroad—a personal and picturesque mode of transport beside the collective and mundane one. The auto freed the traveler from the schedule and course of the railroad and liberated him from its sometimes ugly bordering landscapes. "The motor car has restored the romance of travel," Edith Wharton argued in 1908, "it has given us back the wonder, the adventure, and the novelty which enlivened the way of our grandparents."

But the differences between motor road and railroad touched deeper nerves in the American psyche, which was built on individuals driving and steering themselves through life and society. Hawthorne, in *The Celestial Railroad,* a sort of parody of *Pilgrim's Progress,* depicted railroad culture as a false god, an illusion of salvation. The railroad presents Everyman with the temptation of a free and easy ride to heaven; in fact, of course, it turns out to be an agent of the devil and its destination to damnation.

The automobile, however, put Everyman in the driver's seat and let him choose his own destination. With good roads, the car would become Webster's imaginary railroad where every man can drive his own carriage. And the social and moral implications of the system were revolutionary. "No man with a good car needs to be justified," says Hazel Motes, the deranged evangelist of the "Church Without Christ" found in Flannery O'Connor's *Wise Blood.* Here in brief was the impact of the popular car on rural America and the Bible Belt, touching with that word, "justified," the whole Protestant system. Driving yourself was the very essence of the Protestant ethic, as the fundamentalists knew well who nailed their "Get Right With God" signs on the pine trees beside the road.

THE CAR PRESENTED A DANGER, A TEMPTATION OF ITS OWN, AND IT WAS A RISK THAT EACH DRIVER RAN ALONE.

The political side of this dangerous innovation was clear to some. Woodrow Wilson had feared that the car would make the poor jealous of the rich, but that was before Henry Ford. To many more, the automobile offered a healthy balance to the challenges of godless ideology. Socialism and communism, by the end of World War I and the Red Scare of the early Twenties, were already perceived as threats. The political consequences of the replacement of the railroad by the open road were to be profound.

The social implications of the automobile were clear to the Chevrolet copywriters who created a 1924 magazine ad including these words: "The automobile, fourteen million strong, has in truth become our most numerous common carrier.

"EVERY OWNER IS, IN EFFECT, A RAILROAD PRESIDENT, OPERATING INDIVIDUALLY ON AN ELECTIVE SCHEDULE, OVER HIGHWAYS BUILT AND MAINTAINED CHIEFLY AT THE EXPENSE OF HIMSELF AND HIS FELLOW MOTORISTS.

"What has been the effect of the automobile on our composite national mind? On our social, political, and economic outlook? The once poor laborer and mechanic now drives to the building operation or construction job in his own car. He is now a capitalist, the owner of a taxable asset...

"Evenings and Sundays he takes his family into the country or to the now near town fifty to one hundred miles away. He has become somebody, has a broader and more tolerant view of the one-time cartoon hayseed and the fat-cigared plutocrat. How can Bolshevism flourish in a motorized country having a standard of living and thinking too high to permit the existence of an ignorant, narrow, peasant majority?"

COMMUTERS CROSSING THE TEHACHAPI RIDGE ON HIGHWAY 99. KERN COUNTY, CALIFORNIA.

WITH THE AUTOMOBILE EACH COULD TAKE HIS OWN ROAD, IF NOT NECESSARILY TO HEAVEN OR HELL, AT LEAST TO TOWN. BUT JUST HOW FAR HE COULD GO, OF COURSE, DEPENDED ON THE ROADS.

Good roads became mixed with Babbittry. Good roads would build up Main Street, for wasn't that where everyone was trying to get? Eventually, it was argued, good roads would turn small towns into new Chicagos.

Politicians learned the appeal of road building. In 1912 the federal government at last committed to building roads—under the guise of aiding the postal service. The involvement was part of the populist program to help the farmer and fight the depredations of the railroad on which he was dependent to get his crops to market. And no one accomplished this more thoroughly than populist demagogue Huey Long.

Along the course of Route 84—which runs across the Black River and Little Tensas Bayou and on past the cotton fields and scruffy pine forests of northern Louisiana—are posted thick metal signs with raised letters painted silver. They proclaim that this bridge or that stretch of road "was constructed during the administration of Govs. Huey Long and O. K. Allen." (The signs reminded voters of Long's beneficence. Allen was Long's trusted crony, head of his highway commission and successor as governor.)

More than half a century after those signs were erected, Long is remembered for having built one of the best state road systems in the country, and, better than any politician before him, having seized on the populist political reward of road building.

The first "superhighway" was built in the late Thirties. Actually, it was not a real paved road, but rather a mechanical ride designed to simulate an airplane flight, more specifically, to depict the "future America of 1960." Three hundred twenty-two people sat partially enclosed, in blue velour seats, and were swept along for a fifteen-minute "magic Alladin-like flight through time and space," as the whisper of a recorded narrator called it. You gazed down at models of five hundred thousand buildings, among which streamed some fifty thousand teardrop-shaped cars, and a million trees made of copper wire and Norwegian moss. A machine called the Polyrhetor carefully synchronized that low, intimate narrator's voice—a product of multiple loops of movie sound film—to match the movement of the seats.

As you crossed America, the rosy dusk of the dioramas turned into night, the better to show off the lighting of the landscape, and then, as the "plane" moved across the country past a new Metropolis based loosely on St. Louis, the sun rose again.

But the highlight of the models was the superhighway system: five different lanes in each direction, filled with the tiny cars coursing endlessly, some at fifty, some at seventy-five, some at too many miles-per-hour, crossing from one great freeway onto another by wide, swooping ramps. The whispering voice spoke of crossing America by car within a single day.

Lights embedded in the rails of the highways automatically switched on as automobiles neared them; bridges featured traffic on different levels at different speeds. City and country, industrial and residential areas were neatly divided. Each city block of the metropolis of a million souls, stacked with modern skyscrapers, was "self-contained," while most workers lived in planned suburbs.

At the end of the flight, you stepped onto a rotating circular platform that shunted you to a life-size replica of the intersections in the models: pedestrian bridges over a wide, multilane street for automobiles.

All of this describes, of course, the Highways and Horizons exhibit at General Motors's Futurama: the world of 1960 as seen at the World's Fair of 1939. The Futurama exhibit had more impact than any other single event in acquainting the wider public with the possibilities of superhighways. It was the most popular attraction of the New York World's Fair; as many as ten thousand people might wait two hours or more on any given day to take the fifteen-minute ride. Ten million people eventually visited the 44,000-square-foot, six-million-dollar diorama. The Futurama, as one astute newspaper reviewer put it, combined the "thrills of Coney Island with the glories of Le Corbusier."

The exhibit was designed by Norman Bel Geddes, one of the most flamboyant designers in an era that saw the industrial designer emerge as a public figure, a celebrity, a virtual folk hero of industry. And his "Magic Motorways" helped sell the public and politicians on superhighways.

In October of 1939 General Motors chief Alfred P. Sloan, who had organized a lobby called the American Highway Users Association, held an elegant dinner at the Futurama to court state highway officials and help sell them on the vision of turning Bel Geddes's "Magic Motorways" into reality. Those motorways would make more room, of course, for GM cars. Even President Roosevelt invited Bel Geddes to the White House. Within months, he was drawing four bold lines across the map of the United States, and inquiring of the Bureau of Public Roads what it would cost to turn those lines into superhighways. Too much, came the reply.

But just a couple of hundred miles from the Futurama, a real "magic motorway" soon opened. It was the Pennsylvania Turnpike (later known as Interstate 76). The first portion of a system not yet named or devised, it was, nevertheless, America's first superhighway.

On October 1, 1940, just at midnight, the turnpike was opened—a 160-mile-expanse of concrete with 307

bridges and seven tunnels soon touted as the "Eighth Wonder of the World." Built as a Depression make-work program, the Turnpike was a New Deal triumph.

The road was an immediate sensation, so much so, that on Sunday, October 6, traffic jams several miles long built up at the exits. In the first two weeks, an average of ten thousand cars a day paid their tolls. The turnpike shortened Greyhound's Pittsburgh to Harrisburg bus schedule from nine hours to five and a half. Within a year after its opening, commission officials were urging an expansion.

MANY PEOPLE WERE DRIVING ON THE TURNPIKE NOT TO GET SOMEWHERE, BUT JUST FOR THE SAKE OF DRIVING ON IT.

Families would take a Sunday drive to picnic by the roadside or even, the tales have it, on the grassy median. Or to dine at Midway, which took its name from its location on the pike and had become as festive as a carnival midway. There, or at small lunch counters, drivers would find Howard Johnson's famed twenty-eight flavors of ice cream, "frankfurts" in their little squared-off buns and cardboard holders, and fried clams as "sweet as a nut." Upstairs at Midway was a dormitory packed with steel-pipe bunks for thirty-eight truckers, a lounge complete with radio and pinball machine, and a separate lunch counter.

The modern highway inspired motorists to look more closely at the nature around them. "Cool woodsy stretches abound," proclaims one postcard caption. Another card shows not one bit of the actual turnpike but a deep forest of dogwoods, their pinks and whites and greens tinted several notches up in hue. Ordinary folks were inspired to near poetry. "We arrived safely...the high-

AMERICAN GAS. DURING THE
DEPRESSION, EVEN GAS STAIONS HAD
FEW CUSTOMERS.

way was beautiful with its canopy of stars and its many lights," reads the message on another card.

Here, driving would become an aesthetic experience. With its divided lanes, removal of grade-level intersections and limitation of access, the turnpike promised to remove ninety percent of the causes of accidents. The road was designed so that the straightaways could be negotiated at one hundred miles-per-hour and the curves at ninety. But within days the high speeds showed something else: that, as *Fortune* magazine noted, the turnpike was "the first American highway that is better than the American car...It is proof against every road hazard except a fool and his car."

Tires weren't built for the speeds being reached on the twelve-mile straightaway near Carlisle. Soon blowouts caused accidents—and deaths. But the Pennsylvania Turnpike caught the national imagination. It demonstrated the practicality of the superhighway concept and illustrated its deep pull on the American heart and mind.

The Pennsylvania Turnpike and its later successors were inspired in part by the vision of the German Autobahns. They were excellent propaganda and impressive examples of economic and administrative muscle, both to the foreign visitors who toured these German roads by Zeppelin and—despite the fact that only the elite owned automobiles—to the German public as well. Though it was true that the traffic represented chiefly the powerful and well-off, the implied promise of the Autobahn was that ordinary people would soon be driving their own cars on it; cars like Dr. Ferdinand Porsche's prototype Volkswagens.

The Pennsylvania Turnpike offered this promise of accessibility to all. Billing itself as the American "Dream Highway," it was the realized example of the Highways and Horizons exhibition and paralleled many elements of the Autobahn, including the principle of building motels and gas stations based upon the architectural design of the local regions they occupied.

IN THE DUST OF THE ROAD. WORKERS
FROM A GUNPOWDER FACTORY ON THEIR
WAY HOME. CHILDERSBURG, ALABAMA.

At least as important, however, was the wider economic impact that the Autobahn represented. For a country just coming out of the Depression, superhighways were financial morale builders. Construction projects like the turnpike would provide the same economic pump-priming as did the New Deal's make-work programs.

In the short term, highway construction created many needed jobs that boosted American confidence and national pride; in the long term, completed highways increased transportation efficiency, which would ultimately aid American industry.

Economics, defense, and national prestige were the motives that inspired the American superhighways. The irony is that the Interstate system was itself inaccurately sold to the public in the mid-Fifties as a system of "national defense highways" to facilitate movement of men and material and, illusion as cruel as any of the Autobahns, to evacuate cities in the face of imminent nuclear attack.

DAVISON LIMITED HIGHWAY WAS ONE OF THE FIRST FOUR-LANE EXPRESSWAYS TO FEATURE A GREEN MEDIAN STRIP. DETROIT, MICHIGAN.

IT WAS WITH THE LESSONS OF THE AUTOBAHNS, AND THE IMAGES OF A WAR THAT RUINED EUROPEAN CITIES, THAT PRESIDENT DWIGHT EISENHOWER APPROACHED THE BUILDING OF THE INTERSTATE SYSTEM.

The Interstate program was the last New Deal program and the first space program, combining the economic and social ambitions of the former, with the technological and organizational virtuosity, and sense of national prestige and achievement, of the latter. The planners of the system expanded the public works aspect of highway building into a vision of Keynesian pump-priming and economic "fine-tuning," directed under Eisenhower through private industry. They linked the economic vision to a dubious one of national defense. They adapted the aesthetic (and implicitly the social) values of the American parkway tradition to the new suburbia. They looked back to the German Autobahns for standards of beautiful and efficient engineering. And they answered a public demand for the realization of the utopian, technological future outlined by the streamlining visionaries of World's Fairs and Sunday supplements.

The postwar boom sent more and more people onto the road. But the political wrangling delayed the beginning of the highways mapped out in the 1944 interregional highway plans. Toll roads on the model of the Pennsylvania Turnpike flourished in the Northeast, but no grand national plan existed to link them. Then, to get things moving, Eisenhower appointed Lucius Clay in 1954 to head a committee designed to solve "the road problem" and finally get the Interstates going. The appointment was an immediate indication both of Eisenhower's vision of the Interstates as a weapon in the Cold War and of their political ancestry.

Eisenhower also saw the Interstate as a demonstration of the "right way" to manage the economy, an appropriately Republican version of a Keynesian program. It avoided Roosevelt's "excess condemnation" idea, which came close to expropriation. (The Clay Committee did consider condemnation, but, aside from the major ideological objections, there were administrative problems as well: drawing the line and handling the sales presented opportunities for huge corruption.)

Like Roosevelt in the late Thirties, Eisenhower and his economic advisor, Arthur Bums, saw the Interstate system as a tool to manage the economy. But Eisenhower believed in priming the economic pump with money funneled through the private sector, not in make-work programs like the WPA (Work Projects Administration). If that meant helping big business, so be it; the automobile, directly and

ON THE HIGHWAY TO A METROPOLIS. SERVICE STATION ALONG AN EXIT ROAD. PITTSBURGH, PENNSYLVANIA.

indirectly, accounted for nearly a fifth of the whole economy. Building roads would not add to the efficiency and productivity of that economy, but would aid its largest components directly—the auto makers, of course; the steel, rubber, and plastics industries; and construction. This was a view of internal improvements in the tradition of the Whigs and of Henry Clay's American System.

Eisenhower's views on the matter were not as simple as those credited to his defense secretary, Charles Wilson, formerly of General Motors, to whom was credited the famous line "What's good for General Motors is good for the country." But they were accurately summed up in what Wilson really said: "I've always believed that what was good for the country is good for General Motors, and vice versa."

In addition to the economic impact of its construction, Interstate boosters described the beneficial effects that the highways would have on the ease of operation of the whole economy. Things would move better. Again and again in the arguments in favor of more highways, proponents talked about how a highway "turned space into time." With a fast road you no longer talked about how far you had to go, but about how long it would take you. For commuters, truckers, business travelers, or tourists, the Interstates could, extend the isochrones (lines delimiting the distance one could travel in a given time). If they did not create new places to go, what they did was equivalent in effect. They made it possible to go to more places in the same amount of time.

Eisenhower, too, believed that highways would benefit the whole country. In speaking of the way better highways would provide "greater convenience, greater happiness, and greater standards of living," he echoed widespread public opinion. And there was a clear vision of what sort of living the highways implied. It was the vision of the "American way of life," the summarizing cliché of the Eisenhower Fifties, a decade at whose end the suburban population would equal that of the cities themselves.

When Nikita Khrushchev was planning to visit the United States in the late Fifties, Eisenhower knew just what he wanted to show him: Levittown, a powerful demonstration in Ike's mind of the success of the American system in giving every worker a house as efficiently mass-produced as the car he drove. (Khrushchev, for his part, wanted to see Disneyland.) Part of this success naturally involved highways to get the worker to and from work. The new highway would shorten the time it took to get to the suburbs, effectively expanding the space of the city, trading off space and time in the traditional American manner.

Popular opinion supported this vision, but it was big business that led in mobilizing it. In 1955 the Ford Motor Company published a book called *Freedom of the American Road* boosting road building. It was called "an action book of things you can do" and that included articles by highway boosters from Thomas McDonald to Robert Moses, and showed the benefits of good roads as well as case studies of how "enterprising civic-minded citizens" had gotten new highways built in their localities. The message was that good roads were good Americanism. The appeal was patriotic, boosterish, almost folksy.

HENRY FORD II WROTE IN THE FOREWORD: "WE AMERICANS ALWAYS HAVE LIKED PLENTY OF ELBOW ROOM—FREEDOM TO COME AND GO AS WE PLEASE IN THIS BIG COUNTRY OF OURS."

Lobbying for good roads, Ford wrote, was "democracy in action," and represented typical American resourcefulness.

The "National Defense" tag added to the highway program reflected Eisenhower's background. He came from a new military tradition—the administrative one. He had attended not only the Army War College, but the Army Industrial College. As an officer under MacArthur and Marshall he had become the ultimate aide-de-camp: the soldier as technocrat. His was not only the military that created the logistics miracle of D-Day, but the military that built the Pentagon (a structure served, incidentally, by one of the most modern systems of feeder highways in the world). It was the military of advance planning and of crash programs like the Manhattan Project. This combination of the industrial ethic with the military one was to shape the entire postwar economy. Discouraged at the end of his terms by his struggles with the Pentagon bureaucracy, it was no accident that Eisenhower would popularize the, "military-industrial complex," and like the space program, the Interstate program Eisenhower had promoted was a product of this complex.

The Clay Committee represented the military way of solving the highway problem that the postwar boom had made more acute; it was the way of the "project," the "operation," the "task force." You appointed a task force, worked out a plan of operations, and then launched the project.

The eventual means of financing the Interstate system was the Highway Trust Fund, which quickly became a financial juggernaut on which all the various interest groups had comfortable seats. It assumed the same political sanctity enjoyed by Social Security.

Eisenhower was proud of the Interstate legislation. The federal highway administrators soon began to issue statistics illustrating just how dramatic an achievement the program was. It was to be the greatest public works program in history. It would move enough earth to cover the state of Connecticut knee-deep; it would claim enough land in rights of way to equal the acreage of Delaware;

A HIGHWAY FOR ALL SEASONS. SLIPPERY HIGHWAY 101. SAN JUAN BAUTISTA, CALIFORNIA.

SUBURBAN SLUM. DOCUMENTING SOCIAL
CONDITIONS IN TUPELO, MISSISSIPPI.

it would pave a surface equivalent to that of West Virginia. The concrete it consumed would build six sidewalks to the moon; the lumber it needed equaled four-hundred-square-miles of forest; and the drainpipe was enough for the water and sewer systems of six Chicagos.

The Interstates were only a tiny part of the whole national road system, an average of perhaps twenty percent of road spending in the twenty years after the program began, and only two percent of the total mileage, but they became the model for new highways. The states strove to match their standards. The states had to pay for only ten percent of the Interstate costs, but nearly half of the primary federal aid system, all of their own system costs, and all maintenance costs.

IN MANY STATES,
HIGHWAY BUILDING DURING THE SIXTIES ACCOUNTED FOR WELL OVER HALF OF ALL PUBLIC CAPITAL SPENDING.

While the "National Defense Highway" tag the Eisenhower administration added to the Interstate title was a convenient one in the fearful years of the mid-Fifties, it was also a real part of the scheme. With the threat of atomic warfare looming (the Soviets exploded their first atomic bomb in 1949) it seemed prudent to provide evacuation plans for the cities, even if, privately, officials knew there was no way to accomplish this without advance warning. After participating in a test of the military readiness system, Eisenhower declared the need to work at once on better highways to evacuate the cities.

It was also assumed that in case of war, either nuclear or conventional, the centers of cities would be destroyed by bombing as they had been in Europe. The result was a bizarre combination of incentives—highways to foster the happy, familial, baby-boom suburbs and highways to assist in a potential cataclysmic conflict. And yet somehow they fitted together.

But what the Interstates—like the space program—shared most directly with the military was a system of thought and organization. The Interstates were the apotheosis of that great American love of the project, the program, the system, the module.

Like many such programs, the Interstates took on a bureaucratic and political momentum that was almost impossible to resist. While other transportation needs were neglected, highways, with their unique claim on tax funds, prospered.

But the myth of the Interstates touched on deep American myths—mobility and progress, inner states of cultural longing. Above all, the Interstates were aimed at "keeping America moving." To the engineers, this meant no more than keeping traffic moving; to the interest groups, it meant keeping the flow of their products moving; to the politicians, it had economic, military, patriotic, and almost spiritual implications. The intent of the Interstates was less to bind the country together than to realize an almost mystic principle: to keep things circulating, flowing, to keep the road open.

In 1978, when the last link of I-90, which ran between Boston and Seattle, was completed, a ceremony was held near Blue Lake, Minnesota. The final stretch of highway was marked with gold-painted pavement, an echo of the Golden Spike that completed the Transcontinental Railroad. But the engineers had missed the point. The Interstates were created not so much to bind the nation together as to keep things flowing.

A more relevant ceremony was held in 1984, near the small town of Caldwell, Idaho. On that day, with officials and reporters looking on, "red-eyed Pete," "the last stoplight on the Interstates," was removed, placed in a coffin, and ceremonially buried.

Today, the Interstates are far from universally popular. They are criticized, as were the railroads before them, for offering boring or grim vistas and cutting irresponsibly through cities. Yet a token of the quiet, common inner consensus of their importance can be found in the popularity of the phrase "information superhighway." It implies the idea of providing, electronically, some equivalent of what the superhighway did mechanically with pavement and steel holds.

The excitement once created by the Interstates was now transferred to the Internet. And it was during this time, as traffic began to choke America's highways, that more and more scientists looked at dealing with the congestion by combining these two systems and making the highways electronically smart.

For common citizens however, the impulse was different. If roads were rough and crowded, full of traffic jams and potholes, then they would abandon them. Americans began to buy off-road vehicles with four-wheel drive in unprecedented numbers. In 1995, sports utility vehicles constituted almost half of the country's automotive sales. For most, of course, it was only a dream to leave the pavement, but it was an American dream.

The mid-1990s also saw Americans become obsessed with the expansion and growth possibilities of a different "highway of vision"—the information superhighway, full of potential and capable of updating the dreams and promises fostered by the first Interstates.

There is a neat symbolism to the fact that Al Gore, champion of the Clinton administration's "Information Infrastructure Initiative" for building the information superhighway, is the son of Albert Gore, the Tennessee congressman and senator who helped shepherd the Interstate legislation through Congress in the Fifties. This symbolism illustrates the connection, the parallel, between the superhighway and the information superhighway: both share a set of American dreams of freedom and movement; both tap into an inner state of national longing, and ideal of circulation, communication, grid and network, in which one could happily sing, as the group Talking Heads did, "we're on the road to Nowhere," because Nowhere was also Everywhere. The Interstates did not just traverse physical America, but mapped out a cultural regime as abstract as the cyberspace the Internet linked. They united not only American political states, but the inner states of Americans.

LIGHT AND SHADOW. EXCURSIONISTS
ENJOYING THE BERKSHIRE HILLS. MOHAWK
TRAIL, MASSACHUSETTS.

In 1953, when Los Angeles's freeway system slowly began to grow, two of its new expressways—the one from Harbor to Pasadena and the other from Hollywood to Santa Ana—were linked together in a wholly new and original manner, the interchange. Unlike a highway intersection the interchange is the transposition of lanes and exit and entrance roads to different levels in order to avoid any intersecting at all. This first fully integrated interchange with its three-story bridges, piers, and tunnel-like underpasses was a highway design that was the first of its kind.

The interchange was the vision of freely flowing non-stop traffic. Just as the highway itself, it became a myth of modern times. Contemporaries who drove on it experienced  this traffic, which seemingly regulated itself automatically, as a foretaste to an ideal remote-controlled future world, a piece of highway science fiction.

And yet, a motorist still could not quite take in the extent of these highways, since at the very moment one spots them they are already on top of them. The "transported eye," as Phil Patton refers to this view in his book *Open Road*, must widen its perspective. The best way to see these "cathedrals" of the automobile era is from the window of an airplane, or in a road movie.

In a country where approximately one hundred and fifty million cars and over forty million trucks keep life going, the concept of the freeway has become an agenda. Even traffic jams have something of the grandiose about them when they occur on twelve-lane highways; just the number of tires worn out on them alone would stretch around the equator three times.

Interstate 5 I **Sylmar, California** I 1996

U.S. 66 I **Seligman, Arizona** I 1992   Interstate 10 I **Los Angeles, California** I 1996

Interstate 405 I **Los Angeles, California** I 1996   Interstate 10 I **Los Angeles, California** I 1996   59

"The colonel's face is all over the place," once went a popular saying. The United States has always been the land of unlimited advertising surface; the bearded "Big Brother" who appears on advertisements for the famous chicken fast-food chain is just one example among many. Even the very active Highway Beautification Movement could not succeed against a campaign like the one waged by a famous soft-drink manufacturer, who during the beginning of the century stamped every third house and every fourth tree with its fire-red logo. This proliferation of visual stimuli along expressways and exit roads became a symbol of America— a symbol whose appearance, to be sure, underwent constant change as time went on.

SIGNS

Roadside advertisement has always been able to play the keyboard of American myth with virtuosity—long before the Marlboro Man began riding across the country on advertising billboards the size of cinemascope screens. That was the case for early billboards that were painted directly onto the walls of houses—like the flaked-off beverage advertisement, long since politically incorrect, that makes use of the houseboy cliché of the black butler.

Up until World War II, night driving had been considered dangerous, but in the Fifties, the great period of neon signs arrived. Suddenly, "Times Square" was everywhere. These colorful lighting tubes, which were also popular in the Sixties, are now enjoying a nostalgic revival in the form of smaller-scaled, ready-made neon items. Even the nameless pop artists who take paintbrush in hand aren't dying out. Again and again—like the unknown artist who painted a mini-skirted woman on the exterior wall of his Mexican bar—they continue to create highway icons.

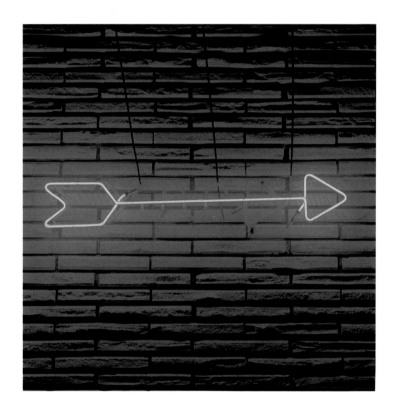

Motel Sign I **Oklahoma** I 1992   Motel Sign I **Beaver, Utah** I 1992

Parking Lot Wall I **Winston-Salem, North Carolina** I 1992   Street Sign I **U.S. 99, California** I 1991

Beginning in 1947, when entrepreneur Frank Urich first hired women on rollerskates to work as cashiers, gas-station business increased considerably. Urich is recognized as the inventor of the self-service station, having taken his inspiration from observing that people at cafeterias always packed more onto their plates than they could eat. He named his service stations, Gaseteria, where a gallon of gas would cost up to ten cents less than at big brand-named stations. His gasoline supermarkets featured up to thirty pumps, served up to two thousand customers a day, and sold up to 130,000 gallons of gas per month—at that time, ten times the amount of an average station.

GAS STATIONS

Self-made men like Urich fought as modern robin hoods against powerful oil companies. The gas wars for cheap prices fought at the roadside represented the fight for mobility and individual freedom. The motorized "go west" momentum, the country's taking of the land in this last century, and the definitive advance of its frontier into the remotest corner was symbolized by the profane institution of the gas station: wherever there stood a gas pump, there was America.

Today, it's all about freedom again. For example, the freedom for nearly one hundred million Americans who commute daily between home and workplace. When the price of gasoline rose as high as $1.60 a gallon in the early summer of 1996 in parts of southern California, it made the headlines of all news reports and newspapers. In an effort to maintain gasoline prices, even cuts in education were proposed by some in government.

Abandoned Gas Station I **Green River, Wyoming** I 1992

Gas-pump Emblem | **Olancha, California** | 1991

Gas Station | **Groom, Texas** | 1991

Fuel Tanker I **San Fernando, California** I 1996   Gas Station I **Rawling, Wyoming** I 1993   67

"Slowly, quietly, and in a dignified manner the big windows of the glass cathedral open, and the faithful enjoy a clear view of priest and preacher." This is how an advertisement describes a drive-in church located in California that was built in 1962 by architect Richard Neutra. Today, churchgoers continue to receive their sermon over their car radios while stationed in a parking lot.

DRIVE INS

In America, where automobiles are an expression of their owners, it is always seen to that not only people but also their cars are well taken care of. One of the service considerations of the age of mobility became the availability of parking. It eventually became superfluous to get out of the car. You merely called in your order through the microphone and received your meal through the side window. The Fifties was an era filled with illuminated drive-in palaces that resembled flying saucers and were characterized—mostly through Hollywood—by young female carhops with colorful little caps topping platinum-blonde perms.

Though the drive-in business is still booming today, the glamour has paled. McDonald's, Wendy's, Burger King, Taco Bell, and KFC & Co. have rationed off the roadside. Gas, Food, Lodging—the trinity composed of gas station, highway restaurant, and motel appears on signs at regular intervals along the highway's edge, continuing to symbolize the basic needs of the man-car symbiosis that are listed at the very top of an unwritten American constitution.

Indeed, there is hardly a need that remains unsatisfied by the drive-in business. Besides the classic roadside entertainments such as drive-in movies and miniature golf—which, unfortunately now struggle in a video society—even the soul can find support along roadside. There is always the palmist who reads the future found on every driver's hand.

Convenience Store | **Oxford, Mississippi** | 1994

Drive-in | **California** | 1992   Hamburger Stand | **Cle Elum, Washington** | 1992

Bordello I **Elko, Nevada** I 1996   Palmreader Sign I **Pismo Beach, California** I 1992

Today, everybody is talking about "community." At a time when there is much lamentation about the decay of values and traditional ties, community is highly sought after, at least it seems that way from talk shows, newspaper articles, and pulpit sermons. The true America lives in the barber shop, the clothing store, the jewelry store, the movie theater, and the drugstore. Mainstreet was the place where everyone still greeted one another by name. In his enormously successful 1920 novel *Main Street,* Sinclair Lewis's realistic depiction of life in a small mid-western town proved a literary memorial to this American icon.

MAINSTREET

Route 66 was called the "Mainstreet of America" partly because it wound through the heart of the country and, in so doing, touched hundreds of little towns and their own mainstreets. But Route 66 was replaced by Interstate freeways, and as they grew, the chances of survival for these small towns decreased. By and by, the barber, the watch-maker, the movie owner, and the druggist closed down their stores. Together with the old highway, the traditional main-street also disappeared, left to exist only as fiction in the collective consciousness.

In many parts of the country, however, there have been successful revitalization efforts to bring it back. Today, in countless small towns, like Ventura, California, many mainstreets have been gentrified and turned into tourist attractions. Second-hand stores and antique dealers have moved in to carry on a trade with America's past. The old, genuine main-street now exists as it once did. Nothing is missing, not the barber shop, the clothing store, the jeweler, the movie theater, or the drugstore.

Walt Disney re-created the mainstreet of his birthplace in Disneyland. Built at two-thirds scale and positioned as the first attraction to greet visitors, it serves as a toy version of America's past.

Mainstreet | **Lindsay, California** | 1995

Mainstreet I **Gallup, New Mexico** I 1992

Mainstreet I **Atwater, California** I 1995

Mainstreet | **Battle Mountain, Nevada** | 1996   Mainstreet | **Kanorado, Colorado** | 1995   75

These children, squinting into the sunset and playing on a frontage road adjacent to Highway 99, aren't vacationing with their parents. They are part of an SSI family living here under government support. This old, cheap hotel was detached from the main traffic by a superhighway, and since then, hardly any vacationers, honeymooners, or traveling salesmen have stopped off. Instead, the municipality relocates needy families into its vacant rooms.

The motel owner shown standing in front of his business is from Bakersfield, California. Born in India, he is the head of a family and represents a typical Gujarati-speaking immigrant, one of many Indians who, during the Seventies, left a bad economy in India with cash in hand to buy up and renovate one run-down motel after another. Indians now manage over seven thousand motels—one out of every three in the United States—and have resuscitated the once-failing motel industry.

Unfortunately, though their lifestyle is often characterized by an adherence to tradition, hard work, and clan loyalty, their ethnic origin sometimes predestines these new citizens to remain outsiders, especially since "real America" is increasingly afraid of being overrun by foreigners.

"Indians represent highway culture, that means lack of culture. It's a no-man's land where they live," says director Mira Nair, who poignantly portrays the problems of this new racism in his 1991 film *Mississippi Masala*. It is a love story set in the sultry south, where time passes sluggishly and many a highway touches on yesterday—a south still reflected here, for example, in the image of a college graduate from Joplin, Missouri, who sells U.S. army surplus items like old military decorations and medals, and a druggist in Natchez, Mississippi, who appears to have lept from the pages of a William Faulkner novel.

Young Woman | **Fresno, California** | 1992

Motel Owner I **Bakersfield, California** I 1992   Druggist I **Natchez, Mississippi** I 1994

Salesman I **Joplin, Missouri** I 1993   Young Boy I **Fresno, California** I 1994   79

At the front door of this garage, there is a sign that says "open," but on the garage door itself, which was once open around the clock, the rust is now peeling off. You can clearly see that it has been closed for a long time; just like Gil's General Store, where dust and melancholy have deposited themselves in the shop window. You can still hear the voices of the children who once came here to buy their ice-cream cones and the accents of the ranchers and oil workers.

A rusty-red track of decay runs through the wealthiest country in the world. Where the odor of transience rises to your nose and faded colors remind you of yesteryear, there

lies the fifty-first state, the realm of ruins. It is everywhere—somewhere on a Californian highway where a defunct diner slowly rots away, or perhaps in New Mexico along a stretch of old Route 66 that now runs into empty space. Or it lies in the expanse of Wisconsin, where wind and weather whistle through thousands of deserted farms.

J. B. Jackson, the "father of cultural geography in America" and a theorist on American popular culture, refers to the "necessity of ruins." By this he means that a society doesn't become aware of its heritage until it threatens to disappear. In the meantime, the Society for Commercial Archeology—an international grassroots organization dedicated to counteracting this threat—has begun its work.

There is no lack of spectacular fields of ruins of popular architecture. In Shamrock, Texas—a once-thriving town now cut off from the Interstates—there are no fewer than fifteen closed-down gas stations represesenting every automotive era, a Pompeii of the gasoline age.

Empty Storefront | **Maricopa, California** | 1992

Abandoned Gas Station | **Shamrock, Texas** | 1992   Abandoned Motel | **Salton City, California** | 1993

Abandoned Cafe | **Bradley, California** | 1993   Sign | **Calexico, California** | 1992   83

Gas Station I **U.S. 40, New Mexico** I 1992

U.S. 101 I **Gilroy, California** I 1994

Neon Sign I **Las Vegas, Nevada** I 1995

Old Factory I **Kansas City, Missouri** I 1995

THE MAIN STREET IS DESERTED. THE ONLY THINGS MOVING ARE SWIRLS OF SNOW...DRIVING AROUND I WILL WASTE MORE TIME.

ROBERT BLY

Diner I **Croton-on-Hudson, New York** I 1991

Bowling Alley Sign I **Missouri** I 1991

Mexican Bar I **Delano, California** I 1991

Mainstreet | **Battle Mountain, Nevada** | 1996

Barber I **Wilkes–Barre, Pennsylvania** I 1995

The Wigwam Motel I **Holbrook, Arizona** I 1991

Sunset Boulevard I **Hollywood, California** I 1996

IN THE WEST THERE ARE MANY ADVERTISING SIGNS, MOVIE FAÇADES, BILLBOARDS, HALF-EATEN AWAY BY THE ELEMENTS, ALREADY FALLING APART. FOR FILMING, I OFTEN CHOSE LOCATIONS THAT I KNEW WOULD SOON DISAPPEAR.

WIM WENDERS

Mainstreet I Battle Mountain, Nevada I 1993

U.S. 66 I **Sayre, Oklahoma** I 1992

Young Boys I **Cleveland, Ohio** I 1995

Warehouse I **Kansas City, Missouri** I 1995

Gas Station I **U.S. 66, California** I 1996

Homeless Shelter I **Bakersfield, California** I 1996

Boulder Highway I **Las Vegas, Nevada** I 1996

BY BERND POLSTER

Los Angeles, March 4, 1928

To the right and left of Santa Monica Boulevard, a vast crowd had gathered. Spellbound, they were waiting for the starting signal. The crowd cheered as the two hundred and seventy-five runners of the International Transcontinental Foot Marathon set off. The participants included an old man with a cane, a Hollywood extra in biblical garb, and a ukulele player who was strumming his instrument while running. The race took them some thirty-five hundred miles straight across the United States, including over the brand new and just half-completed Highway 66. The race was organized by the Route 66 Association, an organization made up of business people and car enthusiasts who had gotten together in order to speed up the construction of the legendary long-distance road.

Even before the start of this mega-marathon, about half a million curious onlookers had gathered. Any community unwilling to lend financial support to the highway project was excluded from the race route. But in small participating towns, at whose gates the world had never before knocked, the runners were welcomed as heroes. For weeks on end, newspapers, weekly news shows, and radio programs fed the nation with news directly from the dusty road—whether it concerned a parched runner crossing the Mojave Desert who was refused a drink of water from a village or another participant who had been side-swiped by a car.

The highway with its curvy but memorable number 66 (which was originally supposed to have been named Highway 60) became the first true national road. Upon finding itself linked up with the East and West, a gasoline company head-quartered in Oklahoma even named its fuel "66." The highway connection between Chicago and Los Angeles would not be completed until the late Thirties, so at the time of the race only about a third of its length of two-lane road had a regular road surface, usually split or concrete. The remaining miles featured only a makeshift surface and had little in common with what we call a highway today. On many desert stretches on the California-Arizona line, cars continued to rattle over wooden planks roughly pieced together. These plank roads, called "corduroy roads," lay across the sandmounds like an endless towel.

There was always something happening along Route 66. The marathon, an enticement with $25,000 in prize money was just one event among many. The Highway Lobby put on a bustling non-stop series of events such as rodeos and Native American shows as well as car exhibits and local fairs. Everything that went on along the new highway was newsworthy. As a result of this continuous advertising display, the highway itself turned into an attraction.

THE HIGHWAY WAS A DESTINATION IN ITSELF. WEEKEND TOURISTS FROM NEIGHBORING TOWNS WOULD CRUISE ALONG IT AND SEND POSTCARDS FROM IT.

Any part of the country that touched this "Mainstreet of America" received a boost. Every advance in construction was carefully documented, especially by the oil and auto industries. Gas stations distributed free road maps. The Texaco Oil Company even published an up-to-date road report that provided details on road conditions.

"The road was a wet black goo transected by deep ruts. The car raced into a morass of prairie gumbo—that is, mud mixed with tar, fish glue, and well-chewed chocolate-covered caramels. When cattle get stuck in this gumbo, the farmers go for stump dynamite." That's how Sinclair Lewis describes a typical American highway in his 1919 novel *Free Air.* Its protagonist, young Milt Pagget, is on the road with his repair shop on wheels and constantly battling the miserable road conditions. "Pull the farmer out of the mud," was a famous slogan of the highway movement.

By the time of the race, the construction of the Lincoln Highway—the first toll-free, all-weather road in America—had already been completed in 1923. Now known as Interstate 80, it traversed the northern half of the United States and its completion had been a national event, despite the fact that it owed its existence in large part to private initiative and sponsor financing. For prior to this construction, even a driver experienced with potholes would need a week or longer to drive from Chicago to New York—provided he didn't get lost on the way.

AS A RULE, UNMARKED AND BARELY KEPT-UP DIRT ROADS CRISS-CROSSED THE COUNTRYSIDE. HARDLY ANYONE COULD IMAGINE THAT THERE WOULD SOON BE A HIGHWAY LEADING FROM ONE END OF THE CONTINENT TO THE OTHER.

A coast-to-coast car trip was an adventure that a doctor by the name of Nelson Jackson, together with his chauffeur,

first accomplished successfully in 1903. The exhausting trip took three months. After that, coast-to-coast trips became the fashion. In 1919, the U.S. Army organized a trek from the East Coast to the West Coast as an advertising campaign for better roads. Prior to their departure, the first milestone was set down on the White House lawn in a solemn ceremony. Forty-two trucks, five cars, as well as a troupe of field-kitchens, tank trucks, and ambulances crept at an average of four miles per hour for about eight weeks from Washington to San Francisco. Despite the slow-going, the objective of the auto-safari demonstration was reached. As President Dwight D. Eisenhower, who had participated in the trek as a young man, reminisced, "The convoy gave me the idea that we should build well-constructed four-lane (speed) highways."

In 1926, *The Family Flivvers to Frisco* became a best seller. An entertaining book describing a trip across the United States from New York, it convinced many people that a transcontinental car trip was no longer dangerous, provided one took certain precautionary measures. Night driving, for example, remained taboo for a long time, since even the largest of potholes couldn't be seen in the dark.

Thus "go west," the adventurous vision of America, had a new driving force. In the Twenties, private associations that supported the highway idea were founded throughout the country. Each saw to it that their own little town would adjoin the highway. According to estimates of the Federal Bureau for Public Roads, by the middle of the decade there were nearly two hundred and fifty marked road segments that also included names given by local associations. Frequently, a single highway was marked with several different symbols simultaneously, often causing drivers to lose their way.

"Here was the nomadic instinct within us popping out in a brand-new form...We were now following the open road...In due time a happy (and quite obvious) solution sprang up in the West and quickly spread throughout the country. This was motor-camping." With these words, a 1921 tour guide explained the new longing to drive out into the green countryside, but modern nomads needed an infrastructure and in 1926, the first motel opened along the stretch between Los Angeles and San Francisco; it offered a parking area, a restaurant, and a coffee shop. Soon, the achievement of mobility was available to everyone, provided they had the finances (and, unfortunately for that time, were also Caucasian.)

According to the *New York Times*, the end of highway romanticism came in the mid-Twenties when Washington officially numbered all the highways sequentially and introduced the standard highway symbol still in use today. Instead of Lincoln Highway or Jefferson Highway—as the first cross-country roads were historically and nostalgically named—there were now austere numbers. The newspaper concluded that "You get no kick out of 46 or 55." As everyone now knows, the paper would eventually be proven wrong and the highways would keep their magic.

Nevertheless, the cultural debate over highways ensued with observers continuing to argue that the opening of the West by means of a network of long-distance roads would sound the death knell of the pioneer spirit. An author would later admonish, in 1928, that where once covered wagons rolled and cowboys "in the wilderness gathered around friendly campfires," there now stood profane "no parking signs along the highway."

The highway symbolized mobility—freedom in geographic, social, and even sexual respects. But to some conservative minds, the countless motels—cheap and anonymous accommodations easily available to couples—represented dens of iniquity, just like drive-in theaters, another innovation of the Thirties where young people could go to gain their first experiences in petting and necking. Author John Steinbeck once said that he thought most Americans had been conceived in the backseat of a Model-T Ford.

Soon there was nothing that couldn't be taken care of in a car, including begging. Vagrants on four wheels were called "motor hobos." The first mobile tramps, they aimlessly cruised along the highway in their decrepit jalopies.

LIKE A MAGNET, THE HIGHWAYS ATTRACTED PEOPLE WHO, DESPITE LITTLE OR NO CAPITAL, STILL POSSESSED A GREAT SPIRIT OF ADVENTURE.

In the Twenties, rapidly increasing traffic promised good business. The new gas stations, motels, restaurants, diners, dance halls, convenience stores, and snack bars that sprung up were mostly family businesses and became the archetypes of the American highway. With "Mom and Pop," you could feel at home even on the road.

Alongside the highway, a totally new phenomenon had cropped up—the roadside business. Many of these drive-in shops were originally located along a town's mainstreet, but, in pursuit of the automobile, they increasingly relocated nearer to the exit roads, transforming these areas into "strips," another American innovation.

By the end of the Twenties, practically all of the roadside institutions known today were already in existence. In deference to the automobile, their newly developed aesthetics followed the law of "speed-reading." That is to say, you had to be able to read the messages from the moving vehicle. For this came the billboards—large advertising walls like those found in Times Square—which now also stood in the open countryside. Architecture and advertisement were intended to stimulate motorists during their brief drive by. Abbreviations that could be read quickly, like "Bar-B-Q," became inexhaustible sources for puns. Motels were named "Ko-Zee," "Sleep U," or "Tour-Rest." The advice to stop for food was reduced to the imperative "Eat."

In 1921, the van de Kamp brothers built a bakery in Los

TRANSPORT LINE. HIGHWAY 99 WAS
ONCE A VITAL TRUCK ROUTE. KERN
COUNTY, CALIFORNIA.

Angeles in the shape of a Dutch windmill. This little shop with its colorful shingles and windmill sails was designed was by Henry Oliver, who later became a famous stage designer in Hollywood. The van de Kamp brothers soon followed this prototype with eighty more such shops. In this glittery town—where people liked Mexican-inspired vernacular architecture—the brothers also built gas stations in the shape of Mexican haciendas. This eye-catching mnemonic style proved ideal for the highway and was adopted by countless anonymous do-it-yourself designers.

Sculptures like oversized ice-cream cones, tea pots, or coffee pots were effective attention-getters for restless clientele. Sometimes the homemade commercial art rose to a classic level, like Mammy's Cupboard in Natchez, Mississippi, a popular tourist cafe built in the shape and likeness of Aunt Jemima.

Among the plaster or paper-maché giants were also trappers and Native Americans as well as a complete zoo, including chickens and dinosaurs. These visual side attractions transformed the highway into a huge fantasy theme park. And long before Walt Disney patented his own fantasies, the creators of these attractions were sensitive to the profit potential of catering to the wishes of children and their easily influenced parents.

In many ways, this naïve roadside art precipitated pop art. This concept of the "vernacular landscape" was also applied to the products of American popular culture. Items such as these have today become the subject of extensive scholarly discussion and are avidly sought after by collectors.

WHETHER AN ADVERTISING POSTER OR THE GLOBE OF A GAS PUMP, ROADSIDE RELICS FROM THE AUTOMOBILE'S EARLY DAYS ARE NOW HIGHLY COVETED COLLECTIBLES AND EARN TOP DOLLAR ON THE NOSTALGIA MARKET.

ICE-CREAM PARLOR ON HIGHWAY 66. THERE WERE NO LIMITS TO THE IMAGINATIONS OF ANONYMOUS ROADSIDE ARCHITECTS. ALBUQUERQUE, NEW MEXICO.

As soon as "roadside" became a concept, it became a theme in American art. Influenced by cubism, Stuart Davis was the first artist to take up this profane subject. It was Davis who for the first time endowed the everyday objects of the consumer with an artistic aura. His oeuvre had the effect of a manifesto on the visual cacophony of modern civilization. This roadside pioneer had no trouble finding form and content in America's rapidly changing urban landscape— last but not least in poster colors and billboard lettering.

In addition, Davis also created an original American iconography with the anthropomorphic gasoline pumps that populated many of his pictures since the early Twenties and which he liked to feature within a setting of small provincial towns. "Already it was deep summer on roadhouse roofs and in front of wayside garages, where new red petrol-pumps sat out in pools of light..." This is just one description among many in *The Great Gatsby* that F. Scott Fitzgerald uses to describe his impressions of a car trip, moving the plot along in an almost film-like manner. Descriptive phrases such as this serve as somewhat of a literary counterpart to the paintings of Stuart Davis.

BIG ACTS. BILLBOARDS FOR MOVIES AND VAUDEVILLE SHOWS ON A SUBURBAN STREET. ATLANTA, GEORGIA.

EDWARD HOPPER, WHO MORE THAN ANYONE ELSE SHAPED "AMERICAN IMAGINATION" (THE TITLE OF A 1995 RETROSPECTIVE) WAS ANOTHER ARTIST WHO REPEATEDLY PAINTED FROM AN AUTOMOTIVE PERSPECTIVE.

Hopper, the master of contrasting light and photo-like images liked to drive through the countryside where he couldn't help but encounter roadside subjects. But whereas they appear as graphic chaos in the paintings by Davis, there is a yawning emptiness in Hopper's works. Gray ribbons of road skim past landscapes and spaces where the few people in it are sad-faced and never speak to each other.

Hopper was satisfied with roads that were swept empty, roads that sometimes served as a backdrop to frozen scenes of simple construction, detailed with people who always seemed to be waiting for something. His work is permeated by a mood of waiting and deep loneliness, as can be seen in his *Western Motel,* which shows a woman sitting beside her suitcases in a room with a view of the street and a car outside; *Four Lane Road* shows a gas station attendant waiting for customers; and *Gas,* depicts a lonely attendant half-hidden in the dusk and working at a pump.

THE HIGHWAY BECOMES A METAPHOR FOR HUMAN EXISTENCE AND ITS ROLE IN THE CONFLICT BETWEEN NATURE AND TECHNOLOGY, SOCIETY AND INDIVIDUAL, RATIONALISM AND ROMANTICISM.

Hollywood also discovered the dark side of the highway early on. In the first film version (made in 1939) of James M. Cain's novel *The Postman Always Rings Twice,* a motel gas station turns into a scene of passion, betrayal, and death. A drifter falls in love with the young, pretty, and bored wife of the owner. Together they conspire to kill her husband. This somber tale of guilt and retribution set in the Depression era was made into a film an additional four times. In his 1960 masterpiece *Psycho,* Alfred Hitchcock also makes use of the roadside milieu as a backdrop for crime. A young woman who has embezzled money from her firm is fleeing on the highway at night. Having taken a room in a run-down motel, she is brutally murdered by its mentally ill owner in what is now one of the most famous murder scenes in the history of film. In 1968, director Peter Bogdanovich portrayed a then new kind of horror in his first film, *Targets,* where a crazed gunman shoots at passing cars, and while trying to flee the police, ends up entrenching himself in a drive-in theater.

GAS GUZZLER. A TRUCKER FILLS UP ONE OF THE TWO FIFTY-GALLON TANKS IN HIS TRUCK. CHARLOTTESVILLE, VIRGINIA.

"HONEST BEER" AND ASPIRIN. A
COUNTER IN A HAMBURGER STAND.
ALPINE, TEXAS.

SOUVENIR SHOP. KITSCHY PICTURES FOR MOTORISTS AT A ROADSIDE BOOTH. CORPUS CHRISTI, TEXAS.

The American roadside also produced a culture shock for non-Americans. In the early Twenties, there were already half a million or so trucks in Los Angeles and the surrounding area, one hundred thousand more than in all of Great Britain. On their return to the Old World, visitors recounting what they had seen would have found it difficult to exaggerate. On a single forty-four-mile stretch of road between Pasadena and San Bernadino, there were at that time over three hundred billboards, one hundred snack bars, and seventy gas stations.

Soon bumper-to-bumper cars, endless concrete expanses, and colorful billboards came to be accepted as quasi-natural elements of the countryside. Nevertheless, the excessive supply of commercialism attacking the human eye from the California roadside—one that became the model for the rest of American roadways—also met with strong reservations. The countryside was now disfigured with thousands of billboards. The poet Ogden Nash made this poetic point: "I think that I shall never see / A billboard lovely as a tree. / Perhaps unless the billboards fall, / I'll never see a tree at all."

As early as 1922 the California Highway Commission had published a report saying that traffic safety didn't depend solely on road conditions. It maintained that roadside "optical pollution" distracted drivers. The newspapers of the day reported on a man who always carried a crowbar in his car in order to immediately tear down the billboards that were being put up along beautiful stretches of highway. In so doing, he cited his "right to see the beauty of the countryside." In 1924 the largest California gas company decided on a spectacular measure. They voluntarily removed more than one thousand billboards from the roadside. Of course this effort to improve the scenery was also in the company's own best interest. Even the National Council for the Protection of Roadside Beauty had determined that "more beauty means more travel. More travel means more gas."

After the Stock Market Crash of 1929, when the automobile boom came to a temporary halt and the United States slid into the biggest economic crisis of the century, Franklin

D. Roosevelt fought the Depression with his gigantic jobs program, the New Deal.

MILLIONS OF DOLLARS WERE POURED INTO PROGRAMS FOR HOUSING AND HIGHWAY CONSTRUCTION; THE GOVERNMENT LEVIED THE FIRST-EVER FEDERAL GASOLINE TAX, OUT OF WHICH NEARLY THREE BILLION DOLLARS FLOWED INTO ROAD CONSTRUCTION.

From 1934 to 1939 the Works Program Administration restored over one hundred and seventy thousand miles of highway. With the aid of these public funds, Los Angeles began the construction of "freeways" (as the first urban expressways were euphorically named).

By the end of the Thirties, long distance highways had become an integral part of American topography. Two Russian artists, Ilya Ilf and Eugene Petrow, traveling in the United States at the time were convinced that "America is located on a large automobile highway." For these visitors from the vast Soviet Union the highways seemed to make the greatest difference to them and made their "journey through America...a voyage over the ocean, monotonous and majestic."

Certainly, Ilf and Petrow summarized the impressions many Europeans took with them upon leaving America: "When we shut our eyes and try to resurrect in memory the country in which we spent four months, we see before us not Washington with its gardens, columns, and a full collection of monuments, not New York with its skyscrapers, its poverty and its wealth, not San Francisco with its steep streets and suspension bridges, not hills, not factories, not canyons, but the crossing of two roads and a gasoline station against the background of telegraph wires and advertising billboards."

BLACK ENTERTAINMENT. A CIRCUS POSTER ON THE WALL OF AN ALABAMA HOUSE.

TO THE COUNTRY THAT WAS THE FIRST TO ADAPT TO THE AUTOMOBILE, THE ROADSIDE HAD BECOME A SYMBOL.

GRAVEYARD SHIFT ON THE HIGHWAY. A SMALL-TOWN GAS STATION WITH GASOLINE STORAGE TANKS. SIKESTONE, MONTANA.

And yet it was already about to change drastically. In order to boost the country's economy, which the crisis had brought to a standstill, American industries began investing in aesthetic packaging. Streamlining became the trend. In the mid-Thirties, star designer Walter Dorwin Teague was hired by Texaco to develop a modern design for the gas station. The most striking characteristics of his design were a simple square form, a generous glass front, and lustrous white façade. Because of the severely cool design and the monolithic style of these buildings, the new gas stations were commonly referred to as "iceboxes."

Introduced in 1937, the new gas station design was a complete success. Not only did it become the most frequently built type of gas station in the country, but for the first time a company also succeeded in representing itself on the highway with an architectural logo. The super-clean "icebox" was a harbinger of the standardized chains of gas stations and fast-food restaurants that relentlessly transformed the image of the American roadside, which, by now, has conquered the exit roads of the rest of the world as well.

In John Steinbeck's novel *The Grapes of Wrath*, the owner of a gas station blusters, "Road is full a people, come in, use water, dirty up the toilet, an' then, by God, they'll steal stuff an' don't buy nothin'. Got no money to buy with. Come beggin' a gallon a petrol to move on." This 1939 best-seller, made into a movie a year later, describes the gas scroungers on U.S. 66 and mythologizes this highway of highways.

The "Mother Road," as Steinbeck referred to it, repre-sented an escape route. Driven from their land by the economic crisis and years of drought, thousands of farmers

IN THE HEAT OF NOON. A GENERAL STORE
ALONG ON A DUSTY ROAD. GORDONTON,
ALABAMA.

from Oklahoma and Arkansas began their trek west. One could recognize them from afar by the mattresses on the roofs of their cars. It was the first automotive migration in world history and an exodus that was extensively documented. Pictures of migrants taken by photographer Dorothea Lange became world famous. To be sure, when these images later reached other parts of the world in the early Fifties, it was hard for some post-war Europeans to believe that people who owned a car could be poor.

WHAT STILL ELICITED ADMIRATION AND AMAZEMENT IN EUROPEAN COUNTRIES LIKE WEST GERMANY—WHERE ONLY THREE OUT OF HUNDRED PEOPLE EVEN OWNED A CAR—WERE NORMAL, EVERYDAY THINGS ON THE OTHER SIDE OF THE ATLANTIC.

During the golden years of the post-World War II decade, as many as nine out of ten American vacationers already used their cars to travel. A trip on U.S. Route 66 was one of the great kicks that even the Smiths and the Joneses could now afford. The highway even lent its philosophy to a highly popular Sixties television series entitled *Route 66* starring George Maharis and Martin Millner. Americans put increasingly more miles behind when traveling by car. They developed a way of driving befitting the land of unlimited miles: "cruising," a relaxed way of gliding over the highway, preferably with suitable music from the car radio and without a clear destination in mind. And when the prairies, mountains, and desertscapes flew past, it was like a watching a movie through the windshield.

The roadside was flourishing, experiencing its greatest and ultimate boom. Soon every little town had its drive-in theater that featured cheap B-movies for teenagers. Neon signs took on superdimensional forms. They became artful creations as voluptuous as the figures of female Hollywood stars—and lighting up the evening sky, they told the stories of a society in love with itself. Motels recycled America's myths with names like Lasso, Golden West, or Astro. The illusion was so perfect that its effects can still be felt today.

American Graffiti, a 1973 Hollywood memoir of the roadside glamour of the Fifties, became a revival classic and paid homage to commonplace teenage games involving roaring engines and sexy drive-in waitresses. In the mid-Fifties the McDonald brothers came up with a cartoon character named "Speedee" to advertise their self-service hamburger chain; and, almost simultaneously, the first standardized "no surprise" motel chain opened—the Holiday Inn. Yet the death knell for the old roadside had begun to sound.

In 1959, German writer Wolfgang Koeppen published *Amerikafahrt* (*American Journey*). Accompanying his themes of the metropolis and of racial segregation, there is a third pervasive theme that characterizes his memoirs. In a society of car lovers, Koeppen, the pedestrian, felt like someone who had been "shipwrecked." He describes not only the functionality—at a motel, for instance, where "people are offered sandwiches and machines are offered fuel"—but also the commercial aesthetics of the American roadside, both of which strike him as trite and monotonous. "Then another mainstreet emerged from the distance and solitude, it always seemed to have been ordered from the same highway factory—as though it had been thrown, ready-made, into infinity, a sudden long row. As always, neon signs were luring, offers and appeals to buy and save were hypnotizing in all the colors of the spectrum. A little Broadway—but behind the colorful, the flickering propaganda signs, there awaited simple one-story houses that had been put there like meaningless decorations."

Koeppen experienced the American highway as a "wondrous landscape" where highways "with six lanes in every direction fly like giant swings through the region of

OCCUPIED. SEVEN lunch customers in a hamburger booth. Harlington, Texas.

BUSY SMALL TOWN. THE MAINSTREET, WHERE REAL LIFE TOOK PLACE. MACON, GEORGIA.

wasted space." He was a witness to the first impressive examples of a new generation of highways, the multilane U.S. Interstates.

The Interstate Highway Act of 1956 called for the installation of a closely-knit highway system across the United States, the biggest road construction project ever conceived in history. With its nearly thirty thousand miles, it was a project of incredible scope as well as great impact on society. In 1950, the first regional shopping mall, Northgate Center, opened north of Seattle and included thousands of parking spaces, about eighty stores, a movie theater, and a service station. In the following years, many cities built similar centers on their periphery, centers whose entry areas had been extended enormously by the Interstates. "Mainstreet," an American institution like cornflakes and the sheriff's badge was now represented by the social vacuum of the mall.

The new express highways and their complicated bypass systems resulted in a frenzy of construction; the most advantageous locations were secured by drive-through industries like oil companies. In 1964 alone, six thousand new gas stations were built, four thousand were modernized, and five thousand were taken out of service. Preferred sites for the new stations were at the intersections of Interstate highways. Gigantic signs were set on poles almost a hundred feet tall to indicate gasoline brands to the driver from a distance. Even service station owners who were cut off from the highway—having been bypassed by the new traffic arteries—erected similar giraffe-necked signs in their distress, but many of them went out of business. And it was not only the off-the-beaten-path gas stations that died off. Nothing but nostalgia remained for most the original highway milieu.

Behind Interstate highways life stood still. Entire cities, such as Shamrock, Texas, grew into modern ghost towns. Thousands of empty shops, rusting gas pumps, and motels with crumbling plaster remained—a landscape of ruins for highway archeologists. Numerous old highways were broken up, many becoming access roads—the so-called

business loops that opened up new commercial areas. Today Route 66, the highway of myth, no longer exists, but the unintimidated still search for the lost past, piece by piece. The classic roadside has vanished, leaving America to grieve its loss.

In 1964 a book appeared with the provocative title *God's Own Junkyard,* and in it America's highways are referred to as "hideous scars on the face of this nation." These scars were seen as being the deserted and monotonous residential streets, the thicket of showy super-advertisements and billboards, the extensive consumers' bunkers along the outskirts, and the sterility of corporate America. This description found an echo in many hearts, especially in the heart of First Lady Ladybird Johnson, the decided enemy of visual robbery who finally took action against it.

IN THE SPRING OF 1966, A YEAR AFTER THE HIGHWAY BEAUTIFICATION ACT DECLARED WAR ON BILLBOARDS AND JUNKYARDS, MRS. JOHNSON INVITED TWO DOZEN OIL MAGNATES TO THE WHITE HOUSE FOR A DISCUSSION.

While the company executives were sipping from their teacups, the First Lady lectured about the much-needed beautification of service stations. Afterwards, they all promised to do their best to improve their appearance, and the result was the new "ranch style" construction of subsequent stations.

In the early Sixties, writers and poets made strong statements over the transformation of the American highway. In 1962, a slim volume with the title *Twenty-six Gasoline Stations* appeared, in which Los Angeles artist Edward Ruscha strung together nondescript photographs of commonplace gas stations. Ruscha's favorite motif consisted of Standard gas stations, with the brand sign as

THROW-AWAY SOCIETY. THE HIGHWAY BEAUTIFICATION MOVEMENT ALSO FOUGHT AGAINST ROADSIDE TRASH. WASHINGTON, D.C.

the only striking element in the picture. In her poem "Filling Station," Elizabeth Bishop onomatopoetically parodies the parade of products in the gas station: "Somebody / arranges the rows of cans / so that they softly say / Esso–so–so–so / to high-strung automobiles." Bishop's poem is a symbol of the standardized environment of a mass-consumer-society, whose profane insignia were artistically sublimated by pop art. Allen Ginsburg's *Hiway Poesy* of the late Sixties tells us about "Red square signs unfold, Texaco Shell / Harvey House tilted over the superhighway."

The interest of pop artists was aroused as well by the uniform signs of the new Interstate highways. Among the new American landscapes were those depicted by Alan D'Arcangelo; stylized views from the perspective of the driver whose gaze is met by gas logos and highway signs. Although long since accepted, like Andy Warhol's *Car Crash* pictures of 1963, they produced shock waves at the time because of their exceedingly commonplace messages.

In 1969, the first film was released in which the highway was the central theme—*Easy Rider*. To some degree, this film paralleled the 1955 novel *On the Road* by beat poet Jack Kerouac. The book was an apotheosis to the freedom of riding that centered on a protagonist who was constantly on the move, though mostly as a fellow passenger who shared gas expenses. It was not until the low budget productions of later Hollywood made it possible to bring this theme of the "dropout" to the screen that the genre of the road movie was established. *Easy Rider* cost only half a million dollars, but netted fifty million and turned its leading actors Peter Fonda, Dennis Hopper, and Jack Nicholson into stars. For the first time, the "on-the-road" feeling was exported worldwide via the movie screen.

"We can't even get into a second-rate motel, because they think we're going to cut their throat or something," says one of the dropouts at the nightly campfire—one of the many scenes reminiscent of the mythical west that offers the opportunity for serious conversation, but over a profane topic, i.e. that long-haired people have to sleep outside.

JUST AS THE OLD HIGHWAY
BECOMES THE GREAT SYMBOL
OF FREEDOM, THE ROADSIDE
STANDS FOR AN UPSTANDING
AMERICA, WHICH REACHES
FOR ITS GUN WHENEVER LAW
AND ORDER ARE THREATENED.

"Get your motor running / Head out on the highway / Looking for adventure / And whatever comes our way." When the motorcycle desperadoes in *Easy Rider* first turn onto the highway, "Born to be Wild" by rock group Steppenwolf resounds. This accompanying music along with the long motorcycle rides shown against a background of expansive scenery, are examples of the significant stylistic influence exerted by this movie. This method of filming, which transposes the myth of the open road into paintings of sound and image, was the cornerstone of the road-movie genre. A more recent film shows that this approach is still effective today. In *Highway 61* (1991), a new-wave version of *Easy Rider*, the action is presented with a cynical wit and involves the transportation of a corpse. Yet at the same time, it is a north to south journey into the history of American music. While the countryside flies past and the center high-way strip is blurred under high speed, the movie seat is transformed into the driver's seat and the screen becomes the windshield.

In the Seventies, the American road movie had high appeal with "crash" addicts and was typified by such films as the trucker movie *Convoy* (1977) by Sam Peckinpah and featured lots of country music. There were also numerous action films that patterned themselves after the 1968 film *Bullitt,* starring Steve McQueen. They routinely incorporated so many highway chases that they were a source of steady employment for many Hollywood stuntmen.

An advertisement for another film, *Vanishing Point* (1971) read: "Within twenty-six hours, he breaks through roadblocks, crucifies policemen, sweeps a jaguar off

RAW MATERIAL FOR THE MORNING PAPER. A TRUCKER IN A NATIONAL FOREST. GRANT COUNTY, OREGON.

HADPINESS smiling by the roadside. The remains of a billboard. Emporia, Kansas.

the road, gets lost in the desert, has a rendezvous with a nude woman on a motorcycle and another one with two bulldozers. And all of it with a lot of music." Completely buried beneath the thriller jargon is the fact that this film is a story portrayed with fascinating photography and combines existential themes with gripping action—without benefit of modern-cowboy romanticism.

In the movie, an ex-racecar driver's flight from the police is turned into the story of a desperate attempt to realize the dream of freedom. Here, too, the highway escape represents an individual's attempt to break away, an attempt that ends in death. The highway thus becomes a symbol of escape from the prison of everyday life.

One of the advantages of the road movie is that new secondary characters can be introduced at any time—characters who may also disappear at any time. Corresponding to this principle of casual encounter are the places where people meet: roadside stores, gas stations, cafes, and motels by the side of the highway, all of which are intended for brief stops only. In these places, communication is merely incidental. The highway is a milieu of superficial encounters. This opens the doors to chance and provides an ideal occasion for dramatic surprises. Moreover, the openness of a situation in which you never know what's going to happen around the next curve is also in keeping with the myth of the open road.

An excellent contemporary film, the 1994 movie *The Chase* derives its tension from the contrast between "everything-is-possible" and "it's-all-over" attitudes. The film begins in a service station where the two protagonists meet. One is an escaped convict so clumsy when holding up a cashier that he is surprised by the police. In his panic, he takes a female customer hostage. During the ensuing chase to the Mexican border, a relationship develops between the convict and hostage. The plot is a contemporary variant on the classic highway drama, since the entire action is being televised live by thrill-seeking reporters.

The road movie requires an endless horizon that is never reached and lonely spots where unusual characters can be found. The highway is a social gray zone. That's why the road movie is an American genre, although it has long since been adopted by Europeans. German filmmakers, too, have ventured out into this area. Yet there is an impression of having to apologize for their main characters' urges to action. Whereas in an American original a strong plot is in the foreground and people get caught up in complicated situations (even in *Easy Rider*, a drug deal provides the occasion for the journey), German protagonists are "flipped out" to begin with as seen, for instance, in the 1993 film *Wir können auch anders* or in *Miss Bolero* of the same year, in which an intense singer named Ninon drives around Chile in a jalopy with no destination in mind. It seems that drifting through life is reserved for outsiders.

In Wim Wenders's 1984 movie, *Paris, Texas* (script by Sam Shepard), the director was able to create something like a meta-roadmovie. He drove around the United States for months in his search of locations. As a result, there is hardly one classic roadside institution left out of this film. On a trip to the desert town of Paris, Texas, neon signs illuminate the nocturnal highway, and even the famous concrete dinosaurs of the Wheel Inn in Cabazon, California, briefly stick their necks into the picture.

OF COURSE, LIKE EVERY GOOD ROAD MOVIE, THE FILM IS ALSO A JOURNEY INTO THE SELF.

And it is also a search for the American Dream, which is juxtaposed here with a realistic impression of America. In a key scene of *Paris, Texas* where the prodigal son chooses his father, the two of them are sitting under gigantic freeway bridges crossing above them, freeways whose brutal architecture also crops up in other parts of the movie.

Paris, Texas was made in the late Seventies, a time when Americans were discovering the vernacular landscape. John Margolies's 1981 book *The End of the Road: Vanishing Highway Architecture in America* was one of the earliest works to concern itself with popular roadside architecture, which at that time was already disappearing. As Wenders said in a later interview, he chose many of the locations for his film "because I knew that they would disappear."

In one of the movie's scenes, two brothers wake up in the morning in Paris, Texas, and find themselves in a ghost town, staring at a rusted automobile wreck. In another scene, they are having a conversation while atop the platform of an enormous billboard that is towering high above a teeming highway and undergoing an advertising slogan change. *Paris, Texas* is an expedition to a land of unrelenting extremes and a commentary on the Americanization of America.

Minorities are depicted chasing after their dreams on the highway as well. In *Stranger Than Paradise*, an early work of Jim Jarmusch from 1984, a hip New Yorker takes his uninitiated cousin from Hungary on a melancholic road trip through America. The 1989 film *Powwow Highway* deals with Native American concerns. The film proceeds slowly, just like the ramshackle used car in which the two leading characters, one activist, one pacifist, chug along from a Montana reservation to Santa Fe. Accompanied by the music of U2 and Creedence Clearwater Revival, they swing across America, encountering and dealing with racism against Native Americans. Music remains an important component even in the modern road movie.

SUDDENLY, IT'S NOT JUST AMERICANS WHO COMPREHEND THAT RIDING ACTUALLY ISN'T ABOUT ARRIVING; THAT FOR MOST OF THE TIME WE REALLY TRAVEL FOR QUITE A DIFFERENT REASON: TO GET AWAY.

The disappearance of the old highway and its living mainstreet has resulted two extremes: one is the concentration of shopping centers and entertainment zones; the other is the mystification of the old highway. With its demise, the highway has become more popular than ever before. Today, places where highway phenomena exist and can be seen have become commercial attractions. The legend of the road has become an export article attracting tourists from around the world.

A favorite destination for Japanese and Europeans on brief vacations is the ultimate consumers' paradise—the Mall of America, the country's largest shopping center located in Bloomington, Minnesota. It is a gigantic world, flashing with chrome and flooded with neon lights, making European shopping centers look like small corner stores. Boasting more than four hundred stores, forty restaurants, fourteen movie theaters, ten merry-go-rounds and two roller coasters, the mall brings in over half a billion dollars annually. There is parking for about fourteen thousand cars in two seven-story parking garages. No driver has to walk further than one hundred yards to the nearest entrance.

Strangely, this trip for shopaholics can be combined with a contrasting itinerary. Some overseas tour organizers also arrange side trips to Route 66 and offer in their brochures the romance of modern ruins and gasoline legends "all expenses included." For less than two thousand dollars, highway addicts can begin at Chicago and traipse along the highway in their rental cars in pursuit of roadside legends.

And when looking back on their trip, those who have enjoyed both the roadside and the brave new consumer world may recollect the slogan taken from *Easy Rider*: "A man went looking for America. And couldn't find it anywhere."

HOPPER ATMOSPHERE. A DESERTED MID-WESTERN HIGHWAY. HARDIN COUNTY, IOWA.

AMERICAN FATA-MORGANA. FAST
FOOD AT A DRIVE-IN BUSINESS.
HOLLYWOOD, CALIFORNIA

HIGHWAY LITERATURE

BAEDER, JOHN:
Gas, Food and Lodging. A Postcard Odyssey Through The Great American Roadside. (Abbeville Press, New York, 1986)
A typical and passionate pictoral trip across early roadside America.

BECKER, JENS PETER:
Das Automobil und die amerikanische Kultur. (WVT, Germany, 1989)
Four wheels roll across America's literature, art, and film.

BEL GEDDES, NORMAN:
Magic Motorways. (Random House, New York, 1940)
The star-designer and Futurama-architect's vision of traffic.

BLAKE, PETER:
God's Own Junkyard: The Planned Deterioration of America's Landscape. (Holt, Rinehart and Winston, New York, 1964)
Sensational documentary that castigates highway construction, commercialism, and the destruction of residential areas.

BRILLIANT, ASHLEIGH:
The Great Car Craze: How Southern California Collided with the Automobile. (Woodbridge Press, Santa Barbara, 1989)
How the West Coast became the cradle of the automobile society.

BRIX, MICHAEL, ET AL.:
Walker Evans. Amerika. Bilder aus den Jahren der Depression. (Schirmer Mosel, Germany, 1990)
Images from the Depression years.

CAIN, JAMES M.:
The Postman Always Rings Twice. (Random House, New York, 1992)
This often-filmed novel originally written in 1934 depicts a roadside drama.

FRANK, ROBERT:
The Americans. (Scalo, New York, 1993)
Frank's black-and-white images, originally published in 1958, had a profound influence on American photography of the Sixties and Seventies.

HOETZEL, HOLGER:
Route 66. Straße der Sehnsucht. (Ullstein Verlag, Germany, 1993)
Route 66: Road of Longing—A German journalist visits the legendary landmarks.

JACKSON, JOHN B.:
Discovering the Vernacular Landscape. (Yale University Press, 1984)
Written by the the "pope" of American popular culture and the inventor of "odology," the science of roads.

JAKLE, JOHN A. & SCULLE, KEITH A.:
The Gas Station in America.
(Johns Hopkins University Press, Baltimore, 1994)
The sociology of a roadside institution, with a sketch about how the "strip" was born.

KELLER, ULRICH:
The Highway as Habitat: A Roy Stryker Documentation 1943–1955.
(University of Washington Press, Santa Barbara, 1986)
Informative study about the origin of the highway and highway photography.

KEROUAC, JACK:
On the Road. (Viking Penguin, New York, 1991)
This "gasoline-permeated" travel journal of the famous beatnik poet was condemned by the critics when first published in 1955.

KOEPPEN, WOLFGANG:
Amerikafahrt. (Suhrkamp Verlag, Germany, 1982)
The author of important economic novels reports about the "New World." First published in 1959.

LEWIS, SINCLAIR:
Free Air. (University of Nebraska Press, Lincoln, 1992)
The portrayer of American society won a Nobel Laureate with this 1919 novel from the pre-highway era.

LYONS, DEBORAH, ET AL.:
Edward Hopper and the American Imagination.
(Whitney Museum of Art/W. W. Norton, New York, 1995)
A collection of Hopper's best-known work combined with a number of critical essays.

LIEBS, CHESTER H.:
Mainstreet to Miracle Mile: American Roadside Architecture.
(Bullfinch Press, Boston, 1985)
Standard work on the history of American roadside architectural classics.

MALCOLM, ANDREW H.:
US 1: America's Original Main Street. (St. Martin's Press, New York, 1991)
Portrait of a highway with an interesting section of black-and-white photographs.

MARGOLIES, JOHN:
The End of the Road: Vanishing Highway Architecture in America.
(Penguin, New York, 1981)
An early work by one of the most famous of roadside research explorers.

MARLING, KARAL ANN:
The Colossus of Roads: Myths and Symbols along the American Highway. (University of Minnesota, Minneapolis, 1984)
America's love for its roadside giants.

MOON, WILLIAM LEAST-HEAT:
Blue Highways: A Journey into America.
(Atlantic Monthly Press, New York, 1983)
The novel about an automobile trip into the core of a civilization.

NABOKOV, VLADIMIR:
Lolita. (Everyman's Library, New York, 1993)
This 1959 novel about a man's love for a minor and the subsequent flight of this unlikely pair takes stock of the American way of life.

NADIS, STEVE, ET AL.:
Car Trouble: A World Resources Institute Guide to the Environment.
(Beacon Press, Boston, 1993)
Diagnosis of the American addiction to automobiles, including suggestions for therapy.

PATTON, PHIL:
Open Road: A Celebration of the American Highway.
(Simon and Schuster, New York, 1986)
A profound history of American superhighways, from the beginning to the present, establishing numerous cultural connections.

POLSTER, BERND:
Super oder Normal. Tankstellen. Die Geschichte eines modernen Mythos. (Dumont Verlag, Germany, 1996)
Super or Regular. Gas Stations: The History of a Modern Myth—the first comprehensive history of gas stations, which also treats the development of American highways and their architecture.

RITTENHOUSE, JACK D.:
A Guide Book to Highway Sixty-Six.
(University of New Mexico Press, Alburquerque, 1989)
This first highway guidebook was originally published in 1946.

SCOTT, QUINTA:
Route 66: The Highway and its People.
(University of Oklahoma Press, Norman, 1988)
A "66-book" that describes its history and everyday life surrounding it.

SILK, GERALD:
Automobile and Culture. (Abrams, Los Angeles, 1984)
The automobile as a work of art and its role in art.

STEINBECK, JOHN:
Grapes of Wrath. (Penguin, New York, 1992)
This 1919 classic novel of social criticism of the Depression became the foundation of the Mother Road myth.

TRIMBLE, MARSHALL:
The Roadside History of Arizona. (Mountain Press, Missoula, 1986)
Nearly five hundred densely printed pages of highway anecdotes.

WALLIS, MICHAEL:
Route 66: The Mother Road. (St. Martin's Press, New York, 1990)
An empathetic text-and-visual essay.

WENDERS, WIM:
Written in the West. (Schirmer Mosel, Germany, 1987)
A contribution to roadside photography by the famous German director.

WILLIAMS, MARK:
Road Movies. The Complete Guide to Cinema on Wheels.
(Proteus Publishing, London, 1982)
The only road-movie monograph to be taken seriously.

YORKE, DOUGLAS A., ET AL.:
Hitting the Road: The Art of the American Road Map.
(Chronicle Books, San Francisco, 1996)
A richly illustrated volume about an American invention.

AN AUTOMOBILE JOURNEY ACROSS AMERICA IS LIKE A JOURNEY ACROSS THE OCEAN, MONOTONOUS AND MAGNIFICENT.

ILYA ILF

Frontage Road) | **Interstate 40, New Mexico** | 1992

Abandoned Motel I **Shamrock, Texas** I 1993

The Capri Motel I **Joplin, Missouri** I 1993

Mainstreet I **Wells, Nevada** I 1996

Motel I **U.S. 66, Missouri** I 1991

BILLBOARDS ARE THE PEOPLE'S ART GALLERY.

BURR L. ROBBINS

Billboard | **Phoenix, Arizona** | 1995

136　　　Bar I **Hollywood, California** I 1996

Mother and Daughter | **Santa Barbara, California** | 1996

Gas Station I **Holbrook, Arizona** I 1992

Truck Driver I **Castaic, California** I 1996

HIGHWAYS, THAT BOLDLY CROSS OVER ONE ANOTHER AND PAIR OFF IN THE MIDDLE OF NOWHERE. CONCRETE VISIONS OF A FUTURE ARCHITECTURE.

WOLFGANG KOEPPEN

Crossing Highways I **U.S. Routes 14 and 5, California** I 1996

The Wheel Inn I **Cabacon, California** I 1992

Patsy's Inn I **Portsmouth, Ohio** I 1995

Tile Store I **New Orleans, Louisiana** I 1994

Alley I **Las Vegas, Nevada** I 1995

HIGHWAY CULTURE, THAT MEANS LACK OF CULTURE. IT'S A
NO-MAN'S-LAND.

MIRA NAIR

The Deep South Motel | **New Orleans, Louisiana** | 1994

ROAD MOVIES

DIE ABFAHRER
(West German, Director: Adolf Winkelmann)
Unemployed juveniles bolt in a stolen moving truck in order to escape from their dismal lives in the Ruhr Valley of Germany.

AMERICAN GRAFFITI
(1973. Director: George Lucas)
The drive-in as meeting place for a clique; problems of adolescence during the babyboomer age. Follows a similar pattern to *American Diner* (1982).

BAGDAD CAFE
(West German, 1988. Director: Percy Adlon)
An offbeat character comedy centered around a German woman who, having walked out on her husband in the middle of the Mojave Desert, finds herself at a dismal Route 66 rest stop.

BONNIE AND CLYDE
(1967. Director: Arthur Penn)
Highway gangsters as folk heroes. The mobile couple engineer bank heists and gas-station robberies in the early Thirties.

BULLITT
(1968. Director: Peter Yates)
The classic high-speed, police-chase movie; contains a single but precedent-setting violent chase scene. The ultimate example in the "clashes-n-crashes" film genre. Films like *Dirty Mary, Crazy Larry* (1974); *The Driver* (1978); and *Deadline Autotheft* (1983) also incorporate high-action chase scenes.

CAR WASH
(1976. Director: Michael Schultz)
Hollywood fluff piece; chief reason for the success of this musical about a typical American roadside business was its funky soundtrack featuring Rose Royce and the Pointer Sisters.

THE CHASE
(1991. Director: Adam Rifkin)
A multilayered highway action drama with unpredictable hairpin-curves. A kidnapping is followed by a horde of TV reporters hungry for sensation. Starring Charlie Sheen and Kristy Swanson.

CONVOY
(1978. Director: Sam Peckinpah)
Highway epic about a good ol' boy trucker who refuses to have his freedom curtailed by either the sherriff or traffic laws. One of the most famous of the trucker movies from the early Seventies that were characterized by tired maxims, dubious trucker romanticism, and country music. Also recommended for fans of fancy driving maneuvers is the box office hit *Smokey and the Bandit,* in which a beer bet leads to insane races and chases. Its success was followed by two sequels and a television series. The worldwide myth of the trucker can be expressed in a loosely staged comedy as in *Impossible...Pas Francais* (French, 1974, Director: Robert Lamoureux) or in a nerve-racking psychothriller like *Road Games* (Australian, 1980, Director: Richard Franklin).

CORVETTE SUMMER
(1978. Director: Matthew Robbins)
A boy, a girl, and a car. The boy from next door sets off for Las Vegas in his souped-up car and meets and falls in love with a call girl working in a bordello-on-wheels. Starring Mark Hamill and Annie Potts.

DUEL
(1971. Director: Steven Spielberg)
In this suspenseful directorial debut by Steven Spielberg, an upstanding motorist is pursued mercilessly by a tanker truck. Neither the driver, played by Dennis Weaver, nor the audience ever get to see the face of the anonmymous trucker.

EASY RIDER
(1969. Director: Dennis Hopper)
L.A. bikers (Dennis Hopper and Peter Fonda) on a trip south in search of America. This low-budget production with its highway rides, its soundtrack, and its depictions of pot-smoking was an expression of a new sense of life and attained cult status.

FASTER, PUSSYCAT, KILL KILL!
(1966. Director: Russ Meyer)
Malicious "Russ Meyer valkyries" race across the Midwest in their sportscar and aggravate hicktown residents.

FROM DUSK TILL DAWN
(1996. Director: Robert Rodriguez)
Trashy flick where policemen get knocked off and hostages are slaughtered. In the TV reports about two escaped convicts played by George Clooney and Quentin Tarantino, the number of people they kill is reported like sports scores. When they enter a strip joint occupied by bloodthirsty vampires, this road movie turns into a orgy of violence.

GAS, FOOD, LODGING
(1992. Director: Allison Anders)
Staged with empathy, this roadside story based on Richard Peck's novel depicts a well-intentioned waitress and her two daughters as they take on the male automotive world.

GRAPES OF WRATH
(1940. Director: John Ford)
Realistic film about the Depression based on John Steinbeck's famous novel. Depicts the exodus of farmers from the Midwest through the Joad family who, in search of a better future, migrate in an old pickup from Oklahoma to California on Highway 66.

HIGHWAY 61
(Canada/Britain, 1991. Director: Bruce McDonald)
This second road movie by McDonald (following *Road Kill*, Canada, 1989), involves a corpse strapped to the roof of a car during a trip down Highway 61 from Ontario, Canada, to New Orleans. Presented as a skillfull mixture of the relationship between an utterly unlikely couple, and thriller gags and dark truths.

HIGHWAY 91
(1988. Director: Jerry Jameson)
Ready-made highway drama: a police inspector tyrannizes innocent drivers.

HIGHWAYMAN
(1987)
This movie about a high-tech agent on eighteen wheels spawned a television series.

HIGHWAY TO HELL
(1991. Director: Ate DeJong)
An automotive "Orpheus" in the Southwest: a young couple, lost in the desert on their way to Las Vegas, get caught up in a phantasmagoric "twilight zone."

HOT ROD GANG
(1958. Director: Lew Landers; Music: Gene Vincent)
All about jeans, pettycoats, and roaring exhaust pipes. An example of Hollywood's teenage, hot rod, beach party, rock 'n' roll B-movies that became drive-in hits. Other movies include *Dragstrip Riot* (1958), *The Lively Set* (1964), and *Hot Rod to Hell* (1967).

IT'S A MAD, MAD, MAD WORLD
(1963. Director: Stanley Kramer)
A half dozen drivers-turned-wild try to trick each other out of a bunch of money they are chasing after. This cynical slapstick road movie, where everything that can go wrong does go wrong, moves along at breakneck speed and features a large cast that includes Spencer Tracy, Milton Berle, Mickey Rooney, Ethel Merman, and Sid Caesar.

JOHNNY DARK
(1954 Director: George Sherman)
An auto maker races from Canada to Mexico in his self-built automobile. Starring Piper Laurie and Tony Curtis. Such stories of racecar drivers have lasting appeal, from *The Crowd Roars* with James Cagney (1932) to *Grand Prix* with Yves Montand (1966; director: John Frankenheimer) to *The Last American Hero* with Jeff Bridges (1973; director: Lamont Johnson)

LENINGRAD COWBOYS GO AMERICA
(Finland/Sweden, 1989. Director: Aki Kaurismäki)
A wandering, rockband from Karelia, Finland, tours the United States going from one god-forsaken place to another, and from one gag to another.

LOLITA
(England, 1962. Director: Stanely Kubrick)
Intense adaptation of Vladimir Nabokov's novel about a man in love with with an underage girl and his constant fear of discovery as he travels throughout the country with her. Starring James Mason and Shelly Winters.

THE LONG, LONG TRAILER
(1953. Director: Vincente Minnelli)
A honeymoon trip in a monstrous trailer satirizes the American way of life.

THE LOVE BUG
(1969. Director: Robert Stevensen)
The first of four Herbie movies from Walt Disney's fairytale workshop. A Volkswagen Beetle turns out to be a magic car, complete with emotions, that rattles drivers on the highway, and includes hilarious scenes such as a two-wheel drive down a curved mountain road. This successful movie concept was also adapted by European filmmakers.

MAXIMUM OVERDRIVE
(1986. Director: Stephen King)
A space catastrophy turns trucks into mechanized murdering horrors. Starring Emilo Estevez.

MISSISSIPPI MASALA
(1991. Director: Mira Nair)
Irreverent comedy of exile about an immigrant family from India that acquires a motel in the South. The themes of love and racism are examined when the daughter falls in love with an African American man played by Denzel Washington.

NORTH BY NORTHWEST
(1959. Director: Alfred Hitchcock)
An unsuspecting Madison Avenue ad executive, played by Cary Grant, is used by the CIA. He experiences a cross-country odyssey as he tries to excape spies and police. Crimes with squealing tires soon became all the rage, as seen in movies like *Thunder Road* with Robert Mitchum (1958; Director: Arthur Ripley), *The French Connection* and *The French Connection II* with Gene Hackman (1971 and 1974; Director: John Frankenheimer), *Trois Hommes A Battre* (French, 1980) and *Prime Target* with Tony Curtis (1991; Director: David Heavener)

OSSESSIONE
(Italy, 1942. Director: Luchino Visconti)
Drama in the dust of the road when a migrant worker finds a job in a gas station, falls passionately in love with the owner's young wife, and together they kill him. Visconti's first film, this milieu-piece was based on James M. Caine's novel *The Postman Always Rings Twice* and was remade in the United States in both 1946 with Lana Turner and John Garfield and in 1981 with Jack Nicholson and Jessica Lange.

PARIS, TEXAS
(West German/French/Italian, 1984. Director: Wim Wender)
Sam Shepard's original and suspenseful story was the model for Wenders's road movie whose images are like metaphors. People traveling on the highway seek, find, and lose each other again. Starring Harry Dean Stanton, Nastassja Kinski, and Dean Stockwell.

PSYCHO
(1960. Director: Alfred Hitchcock)
A young woman fleeing her desperate crime by car encounters the dark side of the highway in a motel setting in this Hitchcock lesson about the unfathomability of souls and shower curtains. Starring Anthony Perkins and Janet Leigh.

REPOMAN
(1984. Director: Alex Cox; Music by Iggy Pop)
A new-wave, Los Angeles character played by Emilio Estevez, who takes a job repossessing automobiles, gets involved with eccentrics and dead aliens. He burns rubber to the accompaniment of Iggy Pop's punk-rock music, while a neutron bomb is ticking in the trunk.

RETURN TO MACON COUNTRY
(1975. Director: Richard Compton)
Highway nostalgia, Fifties-style, in this film with Nick Nolte about teenagers in a souped-up chevy running from trigger-happy cops and fanatical hicks.

ROAD MOVIE
(1973. Director: Joseph Strick)
A truckdriver hauling frozen meat from New Jersey to Chicago quarrels with a woman hitchhiker, which kills both his happy mood and the legend of trucking.

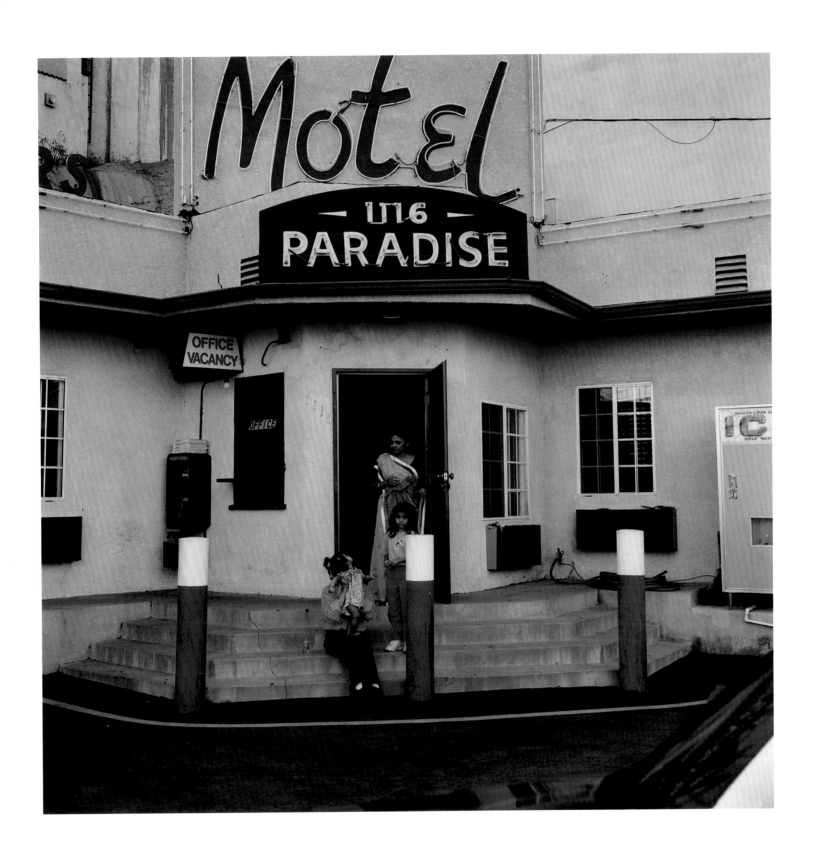

The Paradise Motel | **Los Angeles, California** | 1996

STRANGER THAN PARADISE
(1984. Director: Jim Jarmusch)
A trip to nowhere turns into a depressing automobile odyssey for a couple of young immigrants.

SUGARLAND EXPRESS
(1974. Director: Steven Spielberg)
A couple, wanting the return of their child from the authorities, takes a policeman hostage, and causes a circus of sensation during their flight through Texas that ends in a hail of bullets.

TARGETS
(1968. Director: Peter Bogdanovich)
In this parable about violence, a Vietnam-veteran gun collector methodically shoots innocent drivers on the highway and ends up causing a blood-bath at a drive-in during a horror movie premier. Starring Boris Karloff, and Tim O'Kelly.

THELMA & LOUISE
(1991. Director: Ridely Scott)
Two friends on a weekend excursion end up in a trucker bar. When Thelma is almost raped in the parking lot and Louise shoots the attacker, the women wind up wanted by the F.B.I. Their self-esteem increases as the movie progresses, and the two women never give up, even as their pursuers close in. This movie starring Susan Sarandon and Geena Davis won an Oscar for best screenplay.

TRAFFIC
(French/Italian, 1972)
About cars and people: the smart Mr. Hulot travels from Paris to Amsterdam and faces many obstacles along the way.

TWO-LANE BLACKTOP
(1971. Director: Monte Hellman)
A race between two teenagers in a souped-up '55 Chevy and a blasé middle-aged sportscar driver examines motion as an obsession and an end in itself.

VANISHING POINT
(1971. Director: Richard C. Sarafian)
In this classic road movie, a former race-car driver attempts to take a car from Denver to San Francisco in fifteen hours. Despite the time crunch, he runs into a number of weird people and provokes a chase where anything goes.

WEEKEND
(French, 1967. Director: Jean-Luc Godard)
An "automobile Armeggedon," this movie's ten-minute camera ride alongside a column of cars made film history. Similarly oppressive is the opening scene in *L'Ingorgo* (Italian/French, 1978), and *The Great American Traffic Jam* (1980) where the traffic jam symbolizes the end of time.

THE WILD ONE
(1954. Director: Laslo Benedek)
There were countless sequels to this first movie in which a rebellious motorcycle gang led by Marlon Brando rattles the streets of a quiet town. Among them are such famous and notorious films *The Wild Angels* with Peter Fonda (1966; Director: Roger Corman) and *Hell's Angels on Wheels* with Jack Nicholson (1967; Director: Richard Rush).

WIR KÖNNEN AUCH ANDERS
(German, 1993. Director: Detlev Buck)
In this road movie following German reunification, two people from the former West Germany cross the former German Democratic Republic in a rattled pick-up truck and are mistaken for cold-blooded killers.

ZABRISKIE POINT
(1970. Director: Michelangelo Antonioni)
A student who flees to a parked car-transport truck following a demonstration discovers a girl in a car under him while on U.S. Highway 395. This road movie is transformed into a love story, which, although makes Death Valley bloom, ends tragically.

Motel and Gas Station **Santa Rosa, New Mexico** 1992

THE HIGHWAY WAS THEIR HOME, AND MOVEMENT THEIR MEANS OF EXPRESSION.

JOHN STEINBECK

The Hotel Decatur I **Bakersfield, California** I 1996

Roadside | **Holbrook, Arizona** | 1991

Gas Station I **Cle Elum, Washington** I 1992

Motel Sign I **Lincoln, Nebraska** I 1993

U.S. 66 I **Chicago, Illinois** I 1992

I'D LIKE TO DEDICATE THIS BOOK TO MY SON BEN BROUWS:
MAY HE FIND HIS OWN ROAD, IN HIS OWN WAY, AND TRAVEL ITS LENGTH IN PEACE.

Acknowledgments from Jeff Brouws:

Many thanks go to Peggie Jones whose marketing skills got a copy of my *Twenty-six Abandoned Gasoline Stations* into the bookstore of the Los Angeles County Museum of Art where Bernd Polster found it and thus our collaboration began. In Bernd I have found not only a writer, but a stimulating intellect and friend. Over the last decade I have traveled many roads with many friends and fellow photographers. They include Jackie Woods, Pascale Treichler, Katie Mills (whose cultural understanding of "the road" had a profound influence on my work), Adine Maron, Ed Delvers, Pat Barry, Richard Steinheimer, Jeof Spiro, Jesse Alexander, Cathy Maybury, Patricia Chidlaw, Nell Campbell, Ginny Brush, Guy Williams, Ron Hill, Wayne Depperman, S. R. Bush and Ed Gregory. My thanks to all of you for your love and support.

Through the years I've also received some very excellent advice and encouragement at key times when the going was particularly rough. My sincere appreciation to George Thompson at the Center for American Places, and Amy Pastan at the Smithsonian Institute Press. Thanks also to the gang at Richard Armstrong Color Printer (Jim, Catherine, Don Ron, Gina and Doug E) in Santa Barbara, California, for their superb printing and processing facilities. Similarly, a heartfelt thanks to Matt Ingersoll and the Mickmeister at Art Resources for the top-notch framing and matting of my work. Lastly, my deep gratitude is extended to Phil Patton, Mandy Howard, Joachim Blüher, Olaf Meyer (our design angel), Brigitte Ihsen, Thomas Hauffe, Myriam Frericks, Mary Kalamaras, and all the folks at DuMont and Stewart, Tabori & Chang.

Picture Credits: All color photographs are copyright © Jeff Brouws. All black-and-white photographs are copyright © Library of Congress:
(USF = U.S. Farm Security Administration collection; USW = U.S. Office of War Information collection) and were originated between 1936 and 1943:
Esther Bubley: 105 (USW); John Collier: 32 (USW), 37 (USW), 55 (USF); Jack Delano: 39 (USF), 47 (USF),120 (USF); Walker Evans: 46 (USF), 52 (USF), 109 (USF), 113 (USF), 118 (USF); Dorothea Lange: 40 (USF), 43 (USF), 51 (USF), 104 (USF), 107 (USF), 115 (USF), 116 (USF); Russell Lee: 34 (USF), 36 (USF), 41 (USF), 108 (USF), 111 (USF), 112 (USF), 117 (USF), 121 (USF), 125 (USF); Marion Post Wolcott: 38 (USF); Arthur Rothstein: 35 (USF), 124 (USF); John Vachon: 33 (USW), 110 (USW), 114 (USF), 122 (USF). Jacket photo of Jeff Brouws by Jacqueline Woods.

Published and distributed in the U.S. by Stewart, Tabori & Chang,
a division of U.S. Media Holdings, Inc., New York, New York, 10012
Distributed in Canada by General Publishing Co. Ltd., 30 Lesmill Road,
Don Mills, Ontario, Canada M3B 2T6

Library of Congress Cataloging-in-Publication Data:
Brouws, Jeffrey T.
    [Highway.   English]
    Highway : America's endless dream / photographs by Jeff Brouws ;
text by Bernd Polster and Phil Patton.
        p.   cm.
    Includes bibliograpical references.
    ISBN 1-55670-604-9
      1. Roads—United States—History. 2. Roads—United States—Pictorial
works. 3. Roads—Social Aspects—United States. 4. United States Highway 66—History.
I. Polster, Bernd, 1952- . II. Patton, Phil. III. Title.
HE355.B7413 1997
388.1'0973—dc21
                                            96-29586
                                            CIP

Book design: Bernd Polster (Editor); *Graphic design:* Olaf Meyer;
U.S. editor: Mary Kalamaras; *contributing U.S. designer:* Lisa Vaughn;
Translation: Veronika Albrecht-Rodrigues.

Printed in Germany
10 9 8 7 6 5 4 3 2 1